# Christmas
## at Bear's Paw
## Ranch

Eleanor Burns
and the
Quilt in a Day
Staff

*Merry Christmas from the Quilt in a Day Staff*

*Back – Christina, Stella, Anne, Tom, Matt, Derek, Merritt, Chuck, Judy, Baby True,*
*Middle – Gina, Linda, Sandy, Mercilee, Marie, Melody, Linda, LuAnn, Teresa, Luckie, Debbie, Mary,*
*Mary, Sunny, Amie, Dorothy, Peggy*
*Front – Orion, Peanut, Eleanor, Sam, Sue*

First printing April, 2004
Published by Quilt in a Day®, Inc.
1955 Diamond Street, San Marcos, CA 92069
©2004 by Eleanor A. Burns Family Trust

ISBN 1-891776-16-9

Art Director Merritt Voigtlander
Production Artists Marie Harper and Ann Huisman

# Contents

# 'Twas the Night Before Christmas...

'Twas the night before Christmas
And up at the Ranch
Will Eleanor ever get done?
Is there even a chance?

The family is coming
They'll be here by five.
If she keeps this pace up
Will she even survive?

The quilts were all cut
And ready to stitch,
But can she remember
Which fabrics are which?

When out on the gravel
She heard a car roar,
She looked out the window
As the dogs rushed through the door.

She was relieved to see
It was time for some fun.
Judy and Patty are here
To help get the job done.

They laughed and they talked
And went straight to their work
To get it all done
Without going berserk.

Now her mess is gone
And no one would know
Just how hard and fast
She really can sew.

The packages were wrapped
And under the tree.
Everyone smiled as
Kathy laughed with glee.

A stocking for Orion,
A quilt for Grant,
And Mother looks great
In her new Christmas hat.

Bruce got a gold shirt
To go with his Harley.
Brian's new waders
He'll want to use daily.

And we heard El exclaim
As she turned out the light
"Merry Christmas to all
And to all a good night."

By Sue Bouchard

# Supplies

*These are general supplies. Each project lists supplies specifically for that project.*

*Neutral Thread*

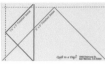
*Small Flying Geese Ruler*

*1½" x 3" and 3" x 6" markings*

*Stiletto*

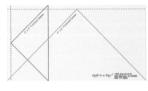
*Large Flying Geese Ruler*

*2" x 4" and 4" x 8" markings*

*¼" Foot*

*6½" Triangle Square Up Ruler*

*Rotary Cutter*

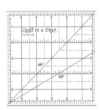
*6" x 12" Ruler*

*6" Square Up Ruler*

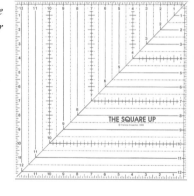
*12½" Square Up Ruler*

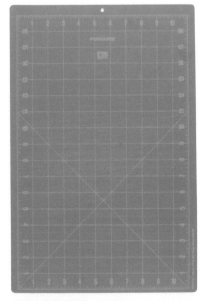
*12" x 18" Cutting Mat*

*6" x 24" Ruler*

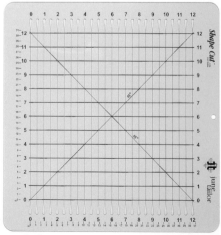
*Shape Cut™*

# Cutting and Sewing Techniques

Each project has a Yardage and Cutting Chart. Follow this example from Tea Cups for selecting and purchasing your fabric, and cutting your strips.

Color coded with pieces in the project; purchase ⅜ yd

Cut two 3" strips for Cup first
  Indented lines under 3" strips indicate pieces cut from 3" strips

Cut three 1½" strips for Cup second
  Indented lines under 1½" strips indicate pieces cut from 1½" strips

*Tea Cups*

## Tea Cups Melissa Varnes
11½" x 14"

### Yardage and Cutting for Four Tea Cups

**Background** — ⅜ yd
Cup
  (2) 3" strips cut into
    (2) 3" x 6" pairs
    (4) 2½" x 5½"
  (3) 1½" strips cut into
    (8) 1½" x 10"
    (4) 1½" x 5½"
    (8) 1½" squares

**Lattice, Border and Binding** — ⅔ yd
  (8) 2½" strips

**Tea Cup** — ½ yd
Cups
  (2) 3" strips cut into
    (2) 3" x 6" pairs
    (5) 3" x 4½" (one for tea bag pocket)

Handle
  (1) 6" strip
Saucer
  (1) 1½" strip cut into
    (4) 1½" x 7"

**One or two 6" doilies cut in half** — ½ yd

**Backing** — 18" x 45"

**Batting**

## Cutting Strips with Ruler

1. Cut a nick in one selvage, a tightly woven edge. Tear across grain from selvage to selvage.

2. Press the fabric, particularly the torn edge.

3. Fold fabric in half, matching frayed edges. Don't worry about selvages not lining up as this is not always possible. Line up the straight of the grain.

4. Place fabric on gridded mat with folded edge along a horizontal line, and torn edge on a vertical line.

5. Place quarter inch line of ruler along torn edge of fabric.

6. Spread your fingers and place four on top of 6" x 24" or 6" x 12" ruler with little finger on edge to keep ruler firmly in place.

7. Take rotary cutter in your free hand and open blade. Starting below fabric, begin cutting away from you, applying pressure on ruler and the cutter. Keep the blade next to the ruler's edge.

8. Cut strips designated widths. Open strip to see if it is straight. If it has a crook that looks like an elbow, the fabric may not be folded on straight of grain. If this happens, repeat preceding steps.

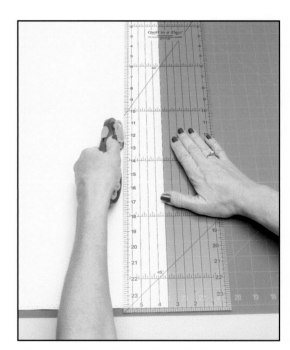

*If you are right-handed, the fabric should trail off to the right.*

*If you are left-handed, the fabric should trail off to the left.*

## Cutting Strips with Shape Cut™

1. Fold fabric into fourths, lining up selvage edges with fold.

2. Place Shape Cut™ on fabric. Line up zero horizontal line with bottom edge of fabric. Allow extra fabric to left of zero for straightening.

3. Place blade of cutter in zero line, and straighten left edge of fabric.

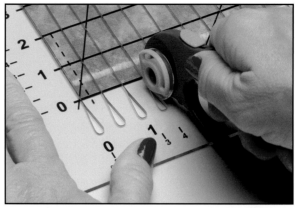

*Line up zero horizontal line with bottom edge of fabric.*

4. Cut strips at designated widths.

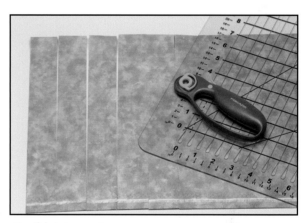

*Cut fabric into strips.*

## Cutting Squares

1. Turn strip, and square off left end.

2. Cut strip into smaller units with 6" Square Up Ruler or 12½" Square Up Ruler, depending on size of pieces.

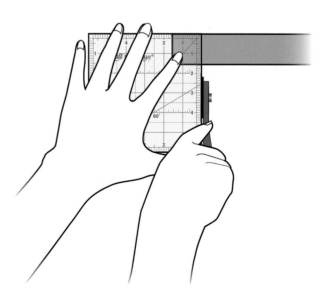

## ¼" Seam Allowance Test

1. Cut three 1½" x 6" pieces.

2. Set machine at 15 stitches per inch, or 2.0 on computerized machines.

3. Sew three strips together lengthwise with what you think is a ¼" seam.

4. Press seams in one direction. Make sure no folds occur at seams.

5. Place sewn sample under a ruler and measure its width. It should measure exactly 3½". If sample measures smaller than 3½", seam is too large. If sample measures larger than 3½", seam is too small. Adjust seam and repeat if necessary.

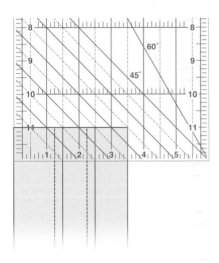

*Use a consistent ¼" seam allowance throughout the construction of your project. If necessary, adjust the needle position, change the presser foot, or feed the fabric under the presser foot to achieve the ¼". Complete the ¼" seam allowance test before starting.*

## ¼" Foot

Available for most sewing machines, a ¼" foot has a guide on it to help you keep your fabric from straying, giving you perfect ¼" seams. Your patchwork is then consistently accurate.

## Needles and Stitch Length

Use a fine, sharp, #70/10 needle.
Use small stitches, approximately 15 per inch, or 2.0 on computerized machines with stitch selections from 1 to 4. Use a machine quilting needle and 10 stitches per inch, or 3.5 on a computerized machine when machine quilting.

## Neutral Thread

Sew the quilt blocks together with a good quality of neutral shade polyester or cotton spun thread. When machine quilting, use the same color thread as the backing in the bobbin and thread the same color as the fabric on top, or invisible thread. Use quilting thread for hand quilting.

## Pressing

*Individual instructions usually say press toward dark, unless otherwise indicated.*

1.  Place on pressing mat, with fabric on top that seam is to be pressed toward. Set seam by pressing stitches.

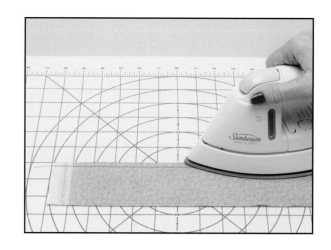

2.  Open and press against seam.

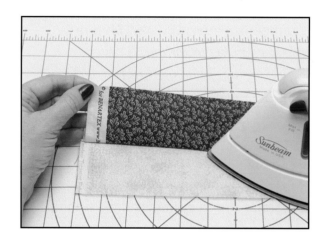

## Measuring and Choosing a Pattern

Decide if you want your quilt to only cover the top mattress, or cover to the floor. Decide if you will tuck the pillows in or use pillow shams on top of the quilt. Measure the length and width of what you want covered on your bed.

On bed quilts in *Christmas at Bear's Paw Ranch*, the blocks cover the top mattress, the first border frames the mattress, and the remaining borders hang over the sides. Check the approximate finished sizes at the top of each yardage chart to find the one that is suited to your purpose. You can always design your own fit by increasing or decreasing the number of blocks and borders.

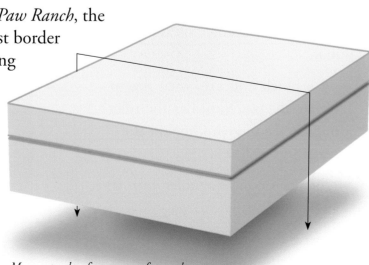

*Measure to edge of top mattress for coverlet size. Measure to floor for bedspread size.*

11

# Using the 6½" Triangle Square Up Ruler

*Projects that use this ruler are:*
*Miniature Star Ornaments*
*Bear's Paw Christmas*
*Saint Nicholas Holiday*
*Any Season Tablerunner*
*Baskets of Cheer*
*Pine Tree Wreath*
*Reach for the Stars*

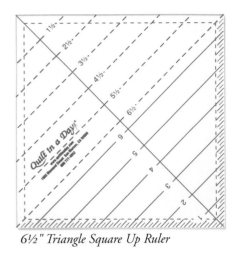

6½" Triangle Square Up Ruler

*Triangles are oversized and need to be trimmed. This technique is called "squaring up." Use the Quilt in a Day 6½" Triangle Square Up Ruler to trim.*

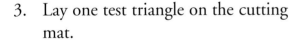

1.  Stack closed triangles light side up. If stitches show better on dark side, stack closed triangles dark side up.

2.  Look for uneven edges. Freshly cut edges don't need to be trimmed. The side with the three stitches was just freshly trimmed, and should be straight. Trim the opposite side.

3.  Lay one test triangle on the cutting mat.

4.  Each block indicates what size to square the patch to. Lay the ruler's indicated square up line **on the seam.**

5.  Line up top edge of ruler with triangle. Hold ruler firmly.

6.  Trim right side of triangle, pushing rotary cutter toward the point to avoid damaging the ruler's corner.

*The example shows squaring the triangle to 2½".*
*The 2½" line on the ruler is on the stitching.*

7. Turn patch. Trim tips with rotary cutter and ruler. From stitching, trim a 45° angle.

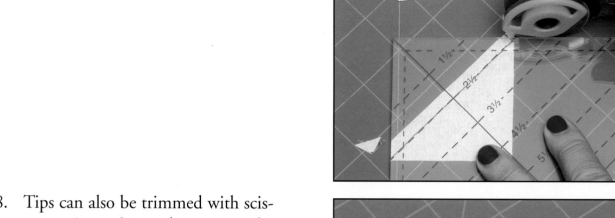

8. Tips can also be trimmed with scissors, using a 60° angle to assure that seam allowance does not show after triangle is pressed open.

   *You can also trim tips after pieced square is pressed open.*

9. Lay trimmed triangle on pressing mat, dark side up. Lift corner and press toward seam with tip of iron, pushing seams to dark triangle side. Press carefully so pieces do not distort.

10. Measure with 6" Square Up Ruler to see if it is desired size. If not correct size, adjust placement of 6½" Triangle Square Up line before stitching if square is too small, or after stitching if square is too large.

# Making Light Star Points or Dark Geese

*Projects that use this technique are:*
*Trees on Any Season Tablerunner*
*Trees on Lone Pine Placemats*
*Stars on Saint Nicholas Holiday*
*Geese on Flying Geese Treeskirt*

1. Place smaller dark square right sides together and centered on larger light square.

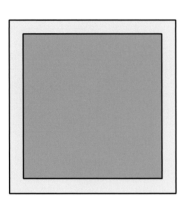

2. Place 6" x 24" ruler on squares so ruler touches all four corners. Draw diagonal line across squares. Pin.

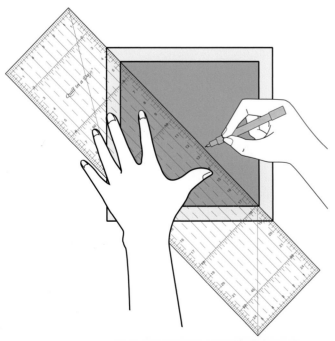

3. Sew **exactly** ¼" from both sides of drawn line. Use 15 stitches per inch or 2.0 on computerized machines. Assembly-line sew several squares. Press to set seam.

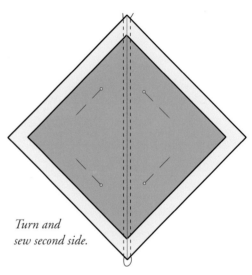

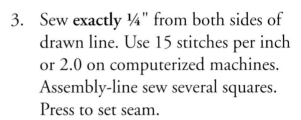

*Turn and sew second side.*

4. Remove pins. Cut on drawn line.

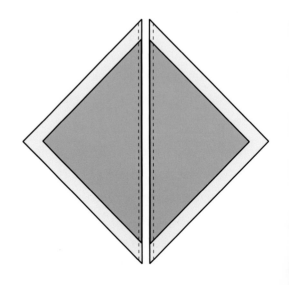

5. Place on pressing mat with **large triangle** on top. Press to set seam.

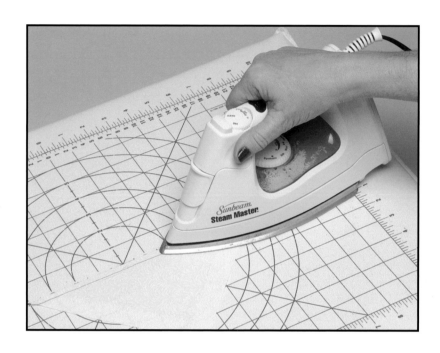

6. Open and press flat. Check that there are no tucks, and **seam is pressed toward larger triangle.**

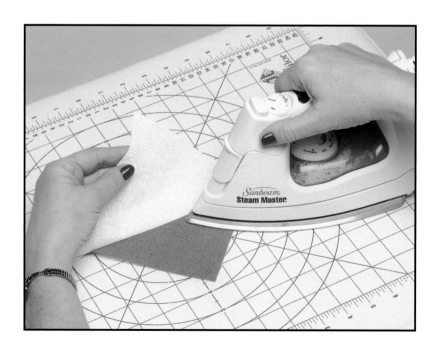

7. Place pieces right sides together so that opposite fabrics touch with dark matched to light.
**Seams are parallel with each other.**

*Seams are pressed toward larger triangle.*

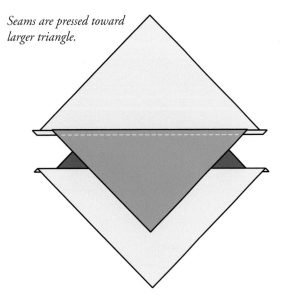

8. Match up outside edges. Notice that there is a gap between seams.
**The seams do not lock.**

*Match outside edges.*

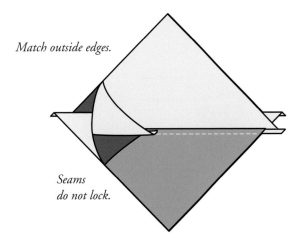

*Seams do not lock.*

9. Draw a diagonal line across seams. Pin. Sew ¼" from both sides of drawn line. Hold seams flat with stiletto so seams do not flip. Press to set seam.

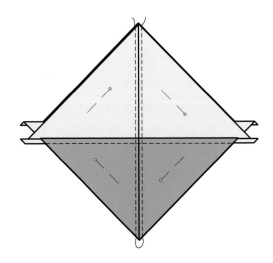

10. Cut on the drawn line.

11. Fold in half and clip to the stitching. This allows the seam allowance to be pressed away from the dark.

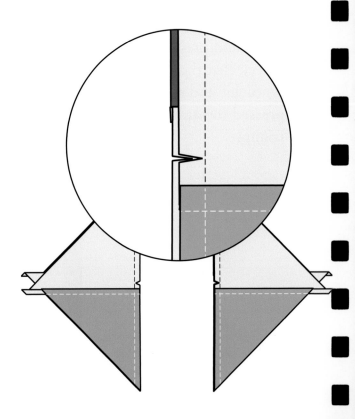

12. From right side, press into one dark. Turn and press into second dark seam.

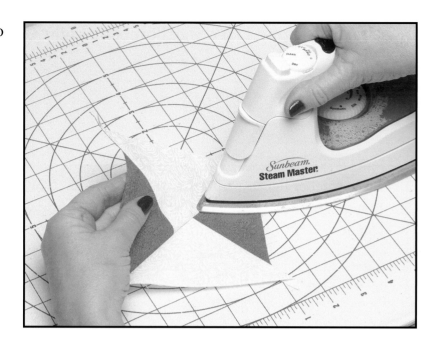

13. Turn over, and press on wrong side. At clipped seam, fabric is pressed away from the dark.

14. Turn to "Squaring Up" directions on pages 21-23.

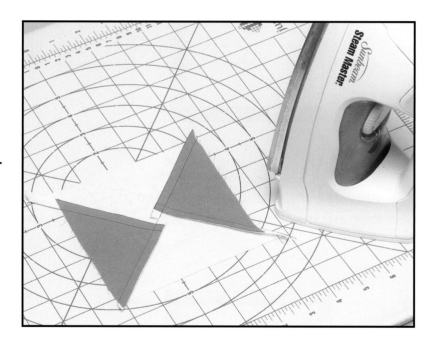

# Making Dark Star Points or Light Geese

*Projects that use this technique are:*
*Stars on Any Season Tablerunner*
*Stars on Reach for the Stars*

1.  Place smaller light square right sides together and centered on larger dark square.

2.  Place 6" x 24" ruler on squares so ruler touches all four corners. Draw diagonal line across squares. Pin.

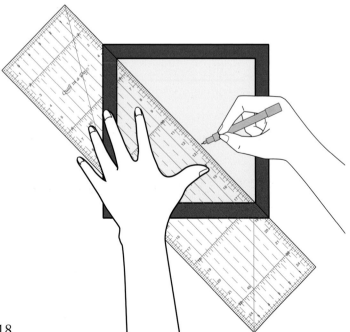

3.  Sew **exactly** ¼" from both sides of drawn line. Use 15 stitches per inch or 2.0 on computerized machines. Assembly-line sew several squares. Press to set seam.

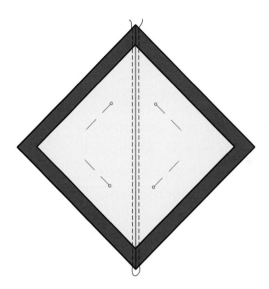

4.  Remove pins. Cut on drawn line.

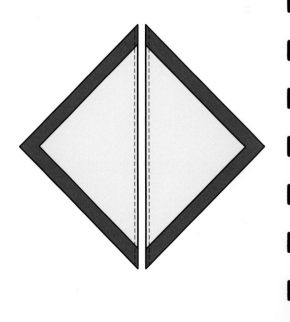

5. Place on pressing mat with **large triangle** on top. Press to set seam.

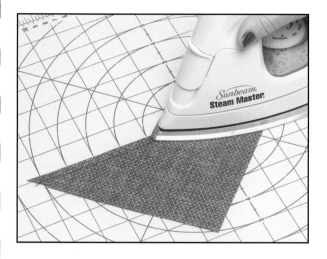

6. Open and press flat. Check that there are no tucks, and **seam is pressed toward larger triangle.**

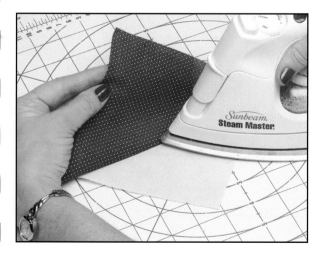

7. Place pieces right sides together so that opposite fabrics touch with dark matched to light. Seams are parallel with each other.

8. Match up outside edges. Notice that there is a gap between seams. **The seams do not match.**

*Seams do not match.*

9. Draw a diagonal line across seams. Pin. Sew ¼" from both sides of drawn line. Hold seams flat with stiletto so seams do not flip. Press to set seam.

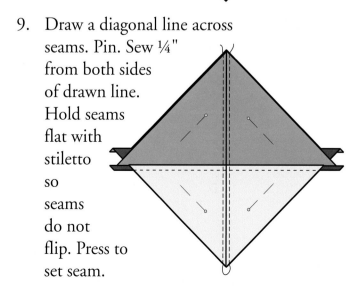

10. Cut on drawn line.

11. Fold in half and clip to stitching. This allows seam allowance to be pressed away from light fabric.

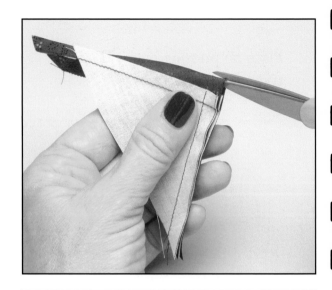

12. From right side, press into one light seam. Turn and press into second light seam.

13. Turn over, and press on wrong side. At clipped seam, fabric is pressed away from light.

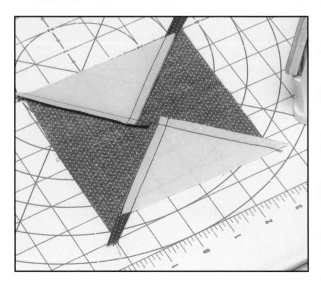

## Squaring Up with Red Lines on Geese Ruler

*If Geese Ruler is unavailable, turn to page 22.*

1. Line up ruler's **red lines** on 45° sewn lines. Line up dotted line with peak of triangle for ¼" seam allowance. Cut block in half to separate two patches.

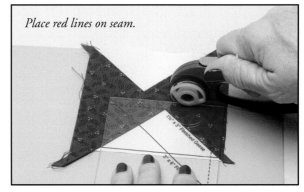

*Place red lines on seam.*

2. Trim off excess fabric on right. Hold ruler securely on fabric so it will not shift while cutting.

*Trim on right.*

3. Turn patch around. **Do not turn ruler.** Trim off excess fabric on right and top.

4. Repeat with second half.

| Trim Size | for | Finished Size |
|---|---|---|
| 2" x 3½" | | 1½" x 3" |
| 2½" x 4½" | | 2" x 4" |

*Turn patch. Trim on right and top.*

## Squaring Up with Green Lines on Geese Ruler

*If Geese Ruler is unavailable, turn to page 23.*

1. Line up ruler's **green lines** on 45° sewn lines. Line up dotted line with peak of triangle for the ¼" seam allowance.

2. Trim excess fabric on all four sides. Turn mat around while trimming.

| Trim Size | for | Finished Size |
|---|---|---|
| 3½" x 6½" | | 3" x 6" |
| 4½" x 8½" | | 4" x 8" |

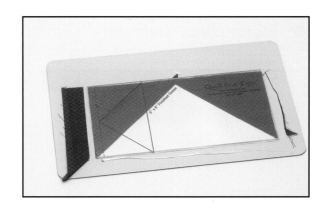

## Squaring Up without Geese Ruler and Red Lines

1. With 6" x 12" Ruler, line up 45° line on a diagonal seam, and ¼" line on peak. Cut across, keeping an exact ¼" seam allowance beyond peak. Turn second piece and repeat.

*Cut block in half. Leave ¼" seam on peak.*

2. With 6" Square Up Ruler, place diagonal line on the seam. Line up bottom edge of patch with designated line on ruler. Trim right and top edges.

| Trim Size | for | Finished Size |
|-----------|-----|---------------|
| 2" x 3½" | | 1½" x 3" |
| 2½" x 4½" | | 2" x 4" |

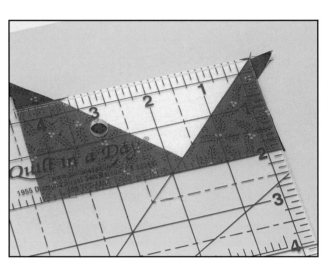

*Example shows trimming a 2" x 3½" patch. Trim off excess fabric on right and top edges.*

3. Turn patch. **Do not turn ruler**. Line up left edge on designated line. Trim on right edge to a perfect size.

4. Repeat with second half.

| Trim Size | for | Finished Size |
|-----------|-----|---------------|
| 2" x 3½" | | 1½" x 3" |
| 2½" x 4½" | | 2" x 4" |

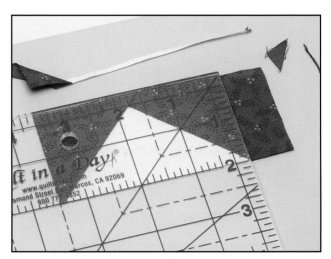

*Turn patch. Trim off excess on right.*

## Squaring Up without Geese Ruler and Green Lines

1. With 6" x 12" Ruler, line up 45° line on diagonal seam, and ¼" line on peak. Cut across, keeping an exact ¼" seam allowance beyond peak. Turn second piece and repeat.

*Cut block in half. Leave ¼" seam on peak.*

2. With 12½" Square Up Ruler, place the diagonal line on seam. Line up bottom edge of patch with designated line on ruler. Trim right and top edge.

| Trim Size | for | Finished Size |
|---|---|---|
| 3½" x 6½" | | 3" x 6" |
| 4½" x 8½" | | 4" x 8" |

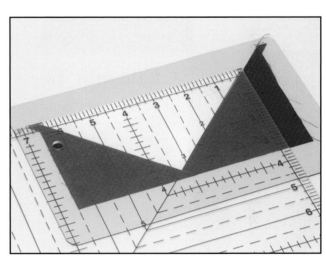

*Example shows trimming a 3½" x 6½" patch. Trim off excess fabric on right and top edges.*

3. Turn patch. **Do not turn ruler**. Line up left edge on designated line. Trim on right edge to a perfect size.

4. Repeat with second half.

| Trim Size | for | Finished Size |
|---|---|---|
| 3½" x 6½" | | 3" x 6" |
| 4½" x 8½" | | 4" x 8" |

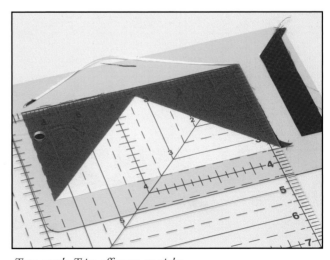

*Turn patch. Trim off excess on right.*

# Children's Projects

Mercilee Searles

Page 34

Linda Parker

## Clothespin Tree

*Every year I enjoy making one holiday project to give to co-workers and friends. These Clothespin Trees are fun and easy. They are a wonderful craft to enjoy with children of all ages. Get creative and give each tree a personality of its own with your unique touches.*

## Chains of Christmas

*On Thanksgiving Day, while wonderful scents floated from the kitchen, the women and children in our family would find the men glued to the television watching football games or on the golf course "bonding." It became our tradition to make a craft and create our own "bonding" experience. We wanted the children to enjoy working with us, so projects were geared for all age levels. A favorite project is the Chains of Christmas. They are quick and easy to make and become a wonderful decoration for the holidays.*

*Happy Holidays!*

Page 26

24

# Patchwork Snowballs

*My mom always saved the wishbone from the turkey for making a Christmas wish. My little sister would cry if she got the short end. So, my mom came up with the tradition that whoever got the short end got married first. Magic — no more tears! All three of us sisters have kept that tradition ever since.*

Amie Potter

Page 30

Amber Varnes

Page 32

# Clay Snowman

*My family and I drive to Abuelita's (Grandmother's) house for Christmas Eve. I just can't wait to be welcomed into a nice, warm house. The smell of Abuelita's Mexican cooking and hot chocolate fills the air. It's the happiest time of the year and cheer is spread all around. All my cousins have a gift exchange. It brings so much delight when we find out who our "secret Santa" is. We all gather together around the Christmas tree waiting for one of my uncles to come in, dressed as Santa, to surprise all the little cousins with presents. The excitement on their faces gives us a warm feeling. I am so happy to share this wonderful time with the ones I love most.*

# Chains of Christmas
## Linda Parker

## Yardage and Cutting for 10' Chain

| Fabric One | ⅓ yd |
|---|---|
| (2) 12" x 22" | |
| Fabric Two | ⅓ yd |
| (2) 12" x 22" | |
| HeatnBond® | 1 yd |
| (2) 12" x 17" | |
| (2) 5" x 12" | |

## Supplies

Fast drying fabric glue

*10' long chain*

## Making Chain

1. Place one 12" x 22" strip of Fabric One wrong side up on ironing board or pressing mat. Lay 12" x 17" strip of HeatnBond®, paper side up, on top. Butt 5" x 12" strip of HeatnBond®, paper side up, to first strip. Press lightly for one to two seconds with dry iron.

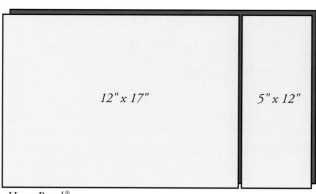

*HeatnBond®*

2. Cool and peel off backing paper.

3. Place second strip of Fabric One on top, right side up. Press for three to five seconds.

4. Repeat steps 1-3 for Fabric Two.

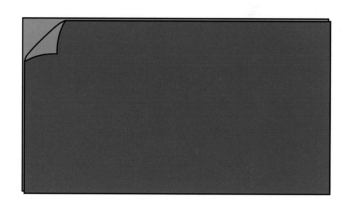

5. Stack bonded Fabric One and Fabric Two. Cut in half into four strips that measure 6" x 22".

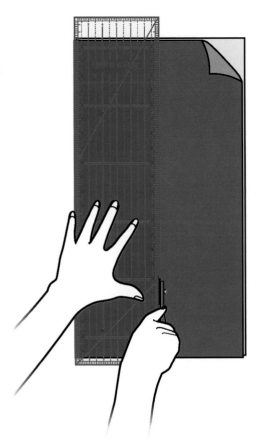

6. Layer cut 6" strips into 1" strips.

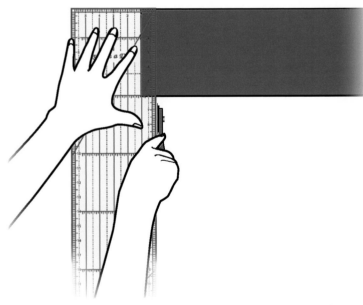

7. Separate Fabric One and Fabric Two into two stacks.

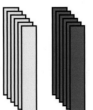

8. Dab glue ¼" from end of strip.

9. Form a ring with Fabric One, overlapping fabric by about ½".

10. Slip a strip of Fabric Two through first link, overlap ends ½" and glue.

11. Alternate until all 6" strips are linked and glued to form fabric chain.

*To store your chain, pack very loosely in an over-sized box.*

# Patchwork Snowballs
## Amie Potter

*3" x 3"*

## Yardage and Cutting

(10) 3" squares of assorted Christmas fabrics per ornament

## Supplies

3" Styrofoam™ balls
12" ribbon per ornament
Wire ornament hangers
Butter or paring knife

## Making Snowballs

1.  Lay first 3" square of fabric on foam ball, right side up.

2.  Using knife, tuck in ¼" edge of fabric all around outside edge into foam ball.

3.  Place second 3" square next to first, and tuck in edges.

4.  Continue tucking in fabric until ball is completely covered.

5.  Stick wire ornament hanger down into foam ball.

6.  Tie ribbon into bow on wire.

# Clay Snowman Amber Varnes

## Materials

| | |
|---|---|
| **Hat** | (1) 1½" clay pot |
| **Hat Brim** | (1) 3" clay tray |
| **Head and Body** | (2) 2½" clay pots |
| **Body** | (1) 3" clay pot |
| **Eyes** | (2) wiggly craft eyes |
| **Scarf** | (1) 2" x 13½" scrap fabric |
| **Buttons** | (3) ⅜" buttons |

## Supplies

Patio Paint™ (will adhere to clay)
    white
    black

Paint or permanent marker
    orange
    pink

Cotton swab

Toothpicks

Low melt hot glue gun

Sponge or paintbrush

*9½" tall*

32

## Painting Snowman

1. Paint 1½" clay pot and 3" clay tray black. Let dry.

2. Paint two 2½" clay pots and 3" clay pot white. Let dry.

*Hat – Black*

*Brim – Black*

## Making Face

1. Dot 2½" face pot with hot glue for eyes. Drop wiggly eyes on hot glue.

2. Apply black paint on toothpick and dot pot for smile.

3. Mark or apply orange paint on toothpick and draw on nose.

4. Mark or apply pink paint to cotton swab and dot rosy cheeks. Let dry.

*Face – White*

## Gluing Body

1. Glue 2½" white pot on top of 3" white pot. Let dry.

2. Take face of Snowman and glue bottom of pot to top of 2½" pot. Let dry.

3. Glue 1½" black pot upside down to 3" black tray, upside down.

4. Glue hat to top of body. Let dry.

5. Glue three buttons in middle for jacket.

6. Fray edges of scrap fabric. Wrap around neck and tie. Glue to hold in place.

7. Let snowman completely dry before handling.

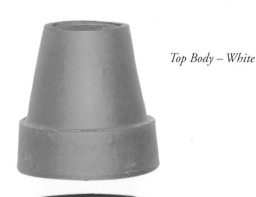

*Top Body – White*

*Bottom Body – White*

# Clothespin Tree Mercilee Searles

*4½" tall*

## Supplies

Wood clothespin

1¼" round wood base from craft store
    (Sold as Doll Pins & Stands)

Short needle artificial tree or short needle garland
    (4) 3¼" branches per tree

Optional Embellishments
    Buttons, string of small ⅜" plastic craft lights

Red marking pen

Low melt hot glue gun

Wire cutters

*Optional
string of
small plastic
craft lights*

## Making Clothespin Tree

1. Paint round base with red marking pen.

2. Glue base to tree with hot glue.

3. Cut garland with wire cutters into four 3¼" branches per tree.

4. Place bowl of cold water close by to dip fingers that might accidentally come in contact with hot glue.

5. Place hot glue at center of one 3¼" branch.

6. Slide down center cut of clothes pin to bottom.

7. Repeat gluing two more branches, spacing evenly. Leave space at top for last piece.

8. Fold last 3¼" piece of garland in half and glue ends into opening, creating a loop.

9. Glue buttons or other embellishments randomly on tree.

10. Use loop to hang on your tree.

*This little tree is also a cute party favor.*

# Tree Decorations

Page 40

Dylan Mayer

## Elf Stocking

*On Christmas morning we all look in the tree to find our own little stocking, filled with a special gift from Santa. Sometimes it is money, but even more special is a note about the upcoming year, like a vacation or special trip to Disneyland®.*

Page 50

## Yo-Yo Garland

Mercilee Searles

*While on jury duty, I started to make a yo-yo tablerunner for Christmas. Once I started to make the yo-yos, I could not stop. The result was this festive yo-yo garland that graces my daughter Nancy's Christmas tree each year.*

## Flying Geese Tree Skirt

Sandy Thompson

*As a young girl, I was lucky to grow up in sunny Southern California. We lived four blocks from the beach. My parents still live in the house where I celebrated my third birthday. Each Christmas seemed to be warm and sunny. After a big meal we all wanted excercise. That's how we started the tradition of walking to the beach after dinner and flying our kites. What a fun thing to do on Christmas Day!*

Sue Bouchard

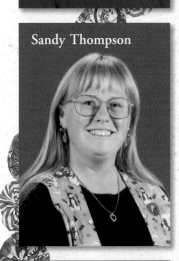

Page 38

Page 44

## Miniature Star Ornaments

Amie Potter

*Sue and I had a magnificent time working together on this project.*

*My parents set up the tree, but it was my responsibility to hang the orna-ments! I enjoyed making ornaments for my family.*

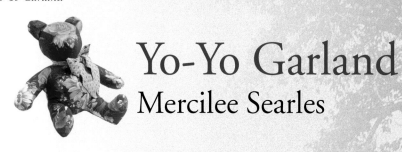

# Yo-Yo Garland
## Mercilee Searles

## Yardage and Cutting for 36" Garland

| Fabrics | 4" circles |
|---|---|

(21) 4" red, white and green circles

*Select red and white prints so yo-yos show on tree branches.*
*Select green prints with light accents.*

## Supplies

Thread

Hand sewing needle

Thimble

Thread Heaven® (thread conditioner)

4" square template plastic

*36" long*

*Pattern found in back of book*

## Making Yo-Yos

1. Find 4" circle on pattern sheet. Trace circle on template plastic and cut out.

2. Trace 4" circles on fabric and cut out.

3. Thread a hand sewing needle with a double strand of matching thread, and knot.

4. Pull thread through Thread Heaven®.

5. From the wrong side, turn under the raw edge ¼" and run a long gathering stitch near the folded edge.

6. Turn right side out, gather tightly, flatten, and adjust gathers.

7. Knot on front side, or push needle through center, and knot on back.

8. Set zig-zag machine stitch to 4.0 mm. Set stitch length to 0.

9. Place two yo-yos side by side.

10. With matching thread and open toe foot, machine sew yo-yos together in long row with wide zig-zag.

11. Continue joining yo-yos to desired length.

12. Optional: Stitch together by hand.

*Black thread is for illustration only.*

# Miniature Star Ornaments
## Sue Bouchard and Amie Potter

*3" x 3"*

## Yardage and Cutting for Six Star Blocks

| Medium | 6" x 9" |
|---|---|

Little Points
   (6) 2½" squares
Centers
   (6) 1" squares

| Dark | 7" x 9" |
|---|---|

Big Points
   (12) 2" squares

| Light Background | 8" x 10" |
|---|---|

Points
   (6) 2½" squares
Corners
   (24) 1" squares

| Dark | ¼ yd |
|---|---|

Border
   (2) 1" strips
Backing
   (6) 3½" squares

| Thin Cotton Batting | 7" x 12" piece |
|---|---|

(6) 3½" squares

| ¼" Ribbon | 1 yd |
|---|---|

(12) 2" pieces

## Supplies

6½" Triangle Square Up Ruler

(60") 18 gauge wire

Invisible thread

Wire cutters

Point turner

Pliers

## Making Six Miniature Stars
*Sew this project with a scant ¼" seam.*

1. Draw two diagonal lines on wrong side of six 2½" Background squares.

2. Place marked 2½" Background squares right sides together with 2½" Little Point squares.

3. Sew scant ¼" seam away from left side of line, across middle, and down right side with scant ¼" seam from line. Use needle down option while sewing patches together. If you don't have this option, manually put needle down while turning squares.

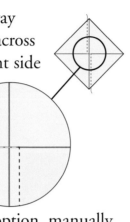

4. Repeat sewing on second diagonal line.

5. Press squares.

6. Cut apart on both drawn lines.

7. Stack triangles with Little Point on top.

8. Trim each seam to ⅛".

9. Press seams toward Little Points.

10. Cut twelve 2" Big Point squares in half on one diagonal.

11. Stack with Little Points. Flip right sides together.

12. Assembly-line sew with scant ¼" seam. Use stiletto to feed pieces through machine. Keep edges together and seams flat.

13. Trim seams to ⅛".

14. Square patch to 1" square. *Place Triangle Square Up Ruler's 1" diagonal line on horizontal stitching line. Place ruler's vertical line on vertical stitches.*

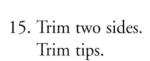

15. Trim two sides. Trim tips.

16. Set seams, open, and press toward Large Points.

# Sewing Star Block Together

1. Lay out patches.

2. Flip middle vertical row to left. Sew vertical row, matching outside edges.

3. Open, and sew right vertical row. Trim seams to ⅛".

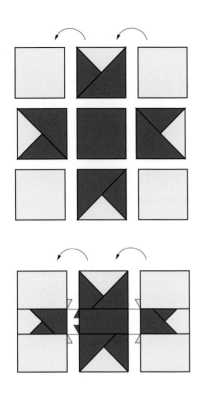

4. Sew remaining rows together, pressing seams toward Corners and Center.

5. Press last rows away from center. Trim seams to ⅛".

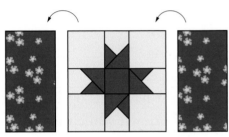

6. Sew 1" Border strips to sides. Press seams toward Border.

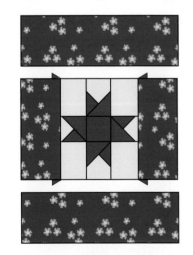

7. Sew 1" Border to top and bottom.

8. Press seams toward Border.

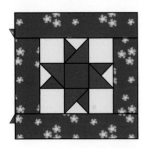

## Finishing

1. To center the loops for ornament, fold 3½" backing square in half, and then in half again. Crease folds with your fingernail.

2. Fold 2" pieces of ribbon in half. Pin to top edge at first and third crease lines on **right side of fabric**.

3. Sew an ⅛" seam across top to anchor loops.

4. Place quilt block on 3½" backing square, right sides together, centering top edge to loops.

5. Place on top of 3½" batting square. Sew ¼" seam around outside edge, leaving a 2" opening to turn.

6. Trim edges ⅛" from seam line.

7. Turn right side out and push out corners with point turner.

8. Tuck in opening, and pin in place.

9. Close opening by hand stitching or, if you choose, machine stitch ⅛" around entire ornament.

10. Stitch in the ditch around Border and Star with invisible thread.

## Making Hanger

1. Cut a 10" piece of 18 gauge wire.

2. Using pattern, loop and curl ends with pliers.

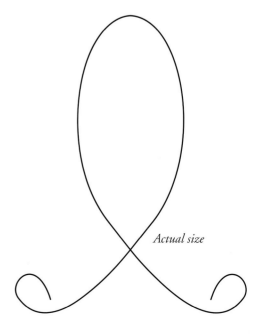

*Actual size*

# Flying Geese Tree Skirt
## Sandy Thompson

*58" x 58"*

## Supplies

6" x 24" Ruler

4" x 8" Flying Geese Ruler

## Yardage and Cutting

| Geese | Twelve different fat quarters |
|---|---|
| (1) 9½" square from each | |
| **Background** | 1¼ yds |
| (4) 11" strips cut into (12) 11" squares | |
| **Lattice** | ¾ yd |
| (8) 2½" strips | |

### Choose One Wide Border

| Border Print | 1¾ yds |
|---|---|
| (4) 5" to 8" wide strips Cut width of stripe x length of fabric into 63" long strips | |

### Or Two Borders

| First Border | ½ yd |
|---|---|
| (6) 2½" strips | |
| **Second Border** | 1¼ yds |
| (6) 6½" strips | |
| **Backing** | 3¾ yds |
| **Batting** | 66" x 66" |

## Making Flying Geese

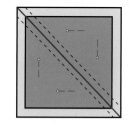

1. Place twelve different 9½" squares right sides together and centered on twelve 11" Background squares.

2. Make forty-eight Flying Geese following instructions beginning on page 14.

3. Square to 4½" x 8½" using green lines on 4" x 8" Flying Geese Ruler.

4. Place four identical Geese in a stack. Make a total of six stacks. Assembly-line sew Geese into pairs.

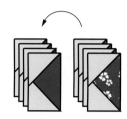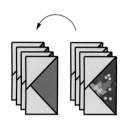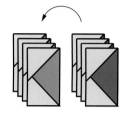

5. Sew three pairs into rows. Make all four rows the same or mix Geese up.

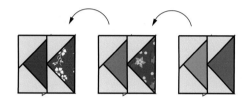

6. Press seams from base toward point.

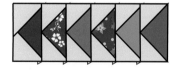

7. Repeat with remaining twenty-four Geese.

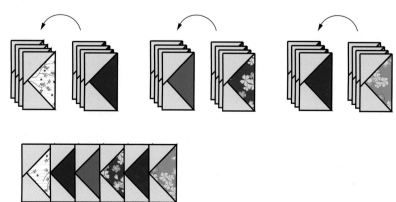

8. Lay out two rows of Geese, with Geese pointing down. Stack a total of four rows on each.

9. Stack four 2½" Lattice strips on left side of each Geese stack.

10. Assembly-line sew Geese to Lattice strips.

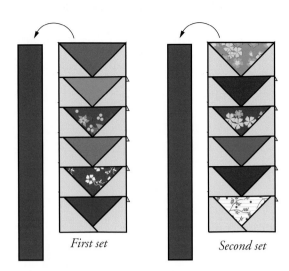

*First set*          *Second set*

11. Set seams, open, and press seams toward Lattice. Square off ends of Lattice.

12. Sew two rows together.

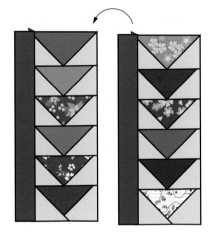

13. Trim Lattice ½" on section that will be left open. *This helps quilt lie flat for quilting.*

14. Sew four sections together, leaving one side open.

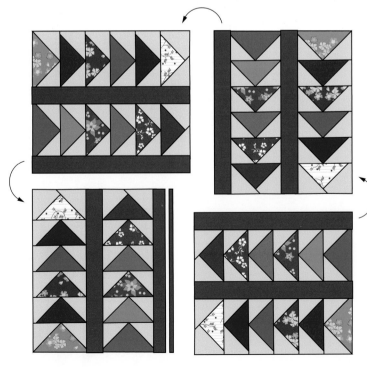

*Leave this side open.*

## Sewing First and Second Borders Together

*Skip this page if using Border Print fabric.*

1. Cut two 2½" First Border strips in half for pieces approximately 20" long.

2. Repeat with two 6½" Second Border strips.

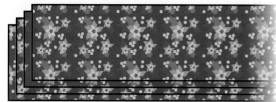

*Two First Border strips cut in half*

*Two Second Border strips cut in half*

3. Sew half strips to ends of four First and Second Border strips so length is approximately 63".

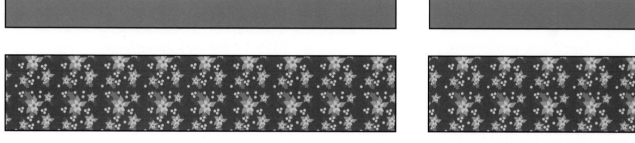

4. Sew four sets of First and Second Border strips together.

5. Press two of each in opposite directions so seams lock at mitered corners.

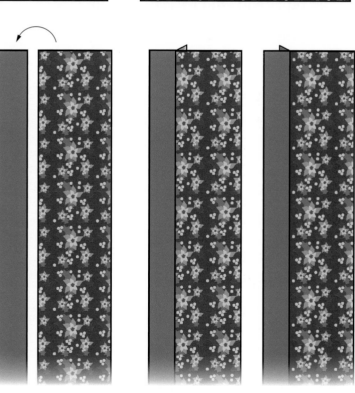

*Press two of each in opposite directions.*

## Sewing Borders for Mitered Corners

1. On **wrong side** of Tree Skirt, mark a dot ¼" in from each corner. Place a pin midpoint on each side.

2. Place a pin midpoint on three Borders.

3. Cut Border next to open seam into a 29" section and a 33" section, and match to opening.

4. Lay Tree Skirt right side up on flat surface.

5. Pin three Borders midpoint right sides together to Tree Skirt midpoints.

6. Pin to ¼" dots on each end.

7. Backstitch to ¼" dot, sew to ¼" dot at other end, and backstitch again.

8. Repeat on all sides.

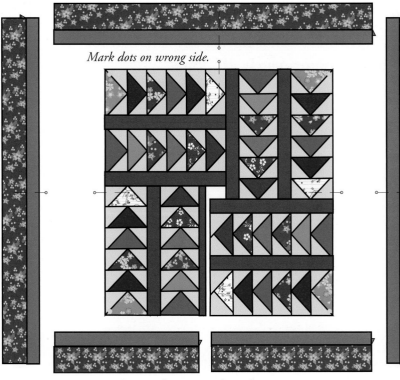

*Mark dots on wrong side.*

*Cut a 29" section and a 33" section.*

9. Fold corner of Tree Skirt and Border extensions diagonally right sides together.

10. Line 45° line on 6" x 24" ruler with edge of Tree Skirt. Match edge of ruler with ¼" dot.

11. Draw diagonal line from ¼" dot to Border edge. Pin.

12. Start sewing exactly at the ¼" point, and stitch on line.

13. Open seam and check.

14. Trim seam to ¼", and press open.

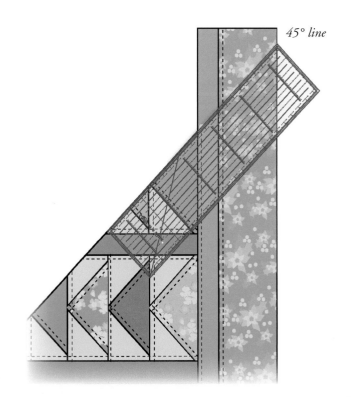

*45° line*

## Finishing with Quick Turn

1. Cut backing into two equal pieces and sew together.

2. Place backing on large table or floor area, right side up.

3. Place Tree Skirt right sides together to backing, and smooth flat.

4. Pin around outside edges and center. Trim backing with 2" extra on each side.

5. Sew around outside edges and center, leaving an opening. See dots. **Do not turn right side out.**

6. Lay out batting and smooth flat. Place Tree Skirt on top of batting. Trim batting and backing to same size as Tree Skirt. Whip stitch batting to seam allowance on Tree Skirt.

7. Turn right side out through opening.

8. Pin opening shut, and whip stitch.

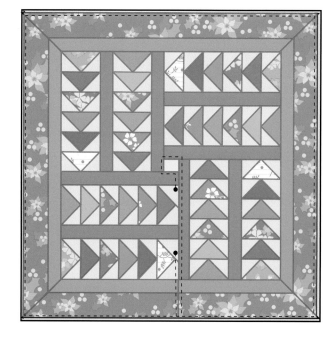

9. Machine quilt by stitching in the ditch through Lattice, Borders, and Geese.

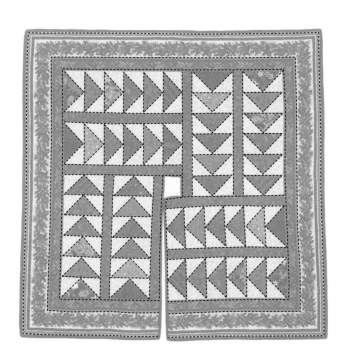

# Elf Stocking
## Dylan Mayer

Use craft felt or wool felt. Pre-wash wool felt in hot water and set dryer on hot. You may need to iron wool felt to get it to lie flat prior to cutting out shapes.

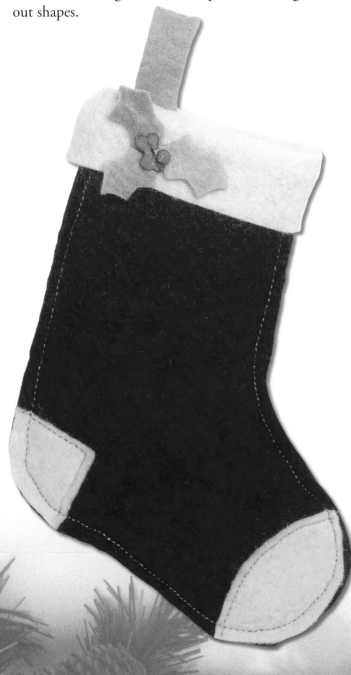

## Yardage and Cutting

| Red Felt | 9" x 12" |
|---|---|
| Stocking | |
| (2) 4½" x 6" | |
| **Off-White Felt** | **9" x 12"** |
| Cuff | |
| (1) 1¼" x 7" | |
| Toe | |
| (1) 1½" x 2½" | |
| Heel | |
| (1) 1" square | |
| **Yellow Felt** | **9" x 12"** |
| Loop | |
| (1) ⅜" x 3½" | |
| **Green Felt** | **9" x 12"** |
| Holly Leaves | |
| (1) 2" square | |

## Supplies

Template plastic

Fabric glue

Red puff paint

Permanent marking pen

*4" x 5"*

*Find patterns in back of book.*

## Making Stockings

1. Trace Elf Stocking from pattern sheet on template plastic, including placement lines for Toe and Heel. Trace Toe pattern on template plastic. Cut out both shapes.

2. Trace two Stocking shapes on red felt with permanent marking pen. Trace Toe on off-white felt. Cut out shapes.

3. Draw tick marks for placement of Toe and Heel.

4. Topstitch Toe and Heel pieces to front Stocking.

5. Using Stocking as a guide, cut off excess Toe and Heel felt.

6. Fold Cuff in half and finger press.

7. Lay Cuff out flat.

8. Pin front and back of Stocking to Cuff with Toes facing each other. Leave ½" between the two. Sew seam with Cuff lying flat.

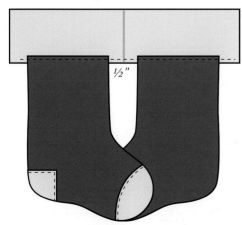

9. Fold loop in half and sew to back of Stocking front.

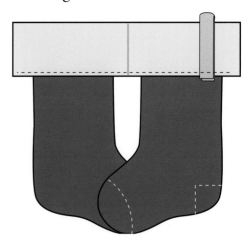

10. Place Stocking front and back wrong sides together. Line up outside edges and sew.

11. Sew edges of Cuff together. Trim off excess. Fold Cuff down over Stocking.

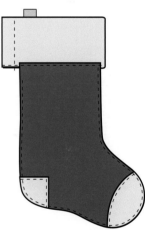

12. Using pattern, cut three Holly Leaves from green felt. Glue on Cuff.

13. Dot Holly Berries with red puff paint.

# Decorative Touches

## Teddy Bear

*For my family, the Christmas season begins on my husband Mike's birthday, December 6. Mike loves the Christmas season! It has become our tradition to set up our live Christmas tree for his birthday. While Melissa and Amber, our daughters, are led by Mike to decorate the tree, I prepare a special dinner for us to share. As a family, we then enjoy the fragrance of the tree and the holiday décor.*

Page 60

Page 70

## Crazy Quilt Stocking

*This project has given me a present. I have never had reason to use the many embellishment stitches on my sewing machine. Trying different stitch numbers and seeing the result was so enjoyable. I love sharing stockings with family and friends.*

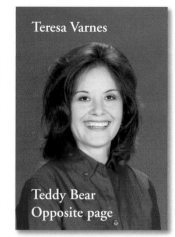

Judy Knoechel

Teresa Varnes

Teddy Bear
Opposite page

Page 54

Eleanor Burns

Luckie Yasukochi

## Strip Stocking

*Strip stockings have been a part of our Christmas celebration for years. When Orion was nine years old, he made a strip stocking for his fourth grade teacher, Mrs. Liska. I remember him standing and sewing at my machine in the dining room while I was cooking dinner. He came running into the kitchen and said, "Oh, Mommie, I love to sew!" May you share the joy of sewing with your children this holiday season.*

Page 64

## Bell and Santa Pillows

*Ever since my first set of twins were born 37 years ago, my parents would come to our house early Christmas morning. After the gifts, a tamale and egg breakfast was traditional. We still have tamales and eggs Christmas morning even though our children have families of their own. The ones that can, come home and spend Christmas morning with their grandparents and mom and dad. Those that can't be here now have tamales and eggs for their Christmas breakfast.*

53

# Crazy Quilt Stocking
## Judy Knoechel

## Yardage and Cutting for One Stocking

| Crazy Quilt Blocks | Ten ¼ yd pieces or Ten fat quarters |
|---|---|
| (1) 7½" square from each | |
| **Thin Cotton Batting** | 16" x 21" |
| | |
| **Muslin Lining** | ½ yd |
| (1) 16" x 42" | |
| **Back** | ½ yd |
| (1) 16" x 21" | |
| **Cuff** | ¼ yd |
| (1) 8" strip | |
| (1) 2" x 6" strip | |

*14" x 17"*
*Find pattern in back of book.*

## Yardage and Cutting for Four Stockings

| Crazy Quilt Blocks | Ten ¼ yd pieces or Ten fat quarters |
|---|---|
| (4) 7½" squares from each | |
| **Thin Cotton Batting** | 1 yd |
| (4) 16" x 21" | |
| **Muslin Lining** | 2 yds |
| (4) 16" x 42" | |
| **Back** | 1 yd |
| (4) 16" x 21" | |
| **Cuff** | ⅝ yd |
| (2) 8" strips | |
| (4) 2" x 6" strips | |

## Supplies

Lace scraps

Buttons

Contrasting threads

Tear away stabilizer

## Making the Pattern

1. Locate Crazy Quilt pattern block in pattern section.

2. Photo copy or trace two copies for each stocking.

3. Cut out Crazy Quilt pattern on outside lines.

## Cutting Crazy Quilt Blocks

1. Carefully stack an assortment of five different 7½" fabric squares **right side up** on cutting mat. Place paper pattern on top.

2. With 6" x 12" Ruler and rotary cutter, cut on center line and separate into two halves.

3. Cut on remaining lines.

4. Repeat for second stack of five squares. Remove paper.

5. Stack second pieces on top of first ones. Keep pieces "in square."

6. Mix up patches by separating stacks in different places and putting top of each stack on bottom. Fabric on top of each stack should be different.

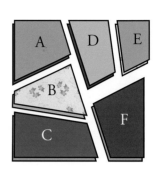

## Sewing Left Side Together

*Pieces do not need to match perfectly. They are sliver trimmed to match during construction, and squared to 5½" once they are completed.*

1. Lay out stacks A and B. Flip B right sides together to A.

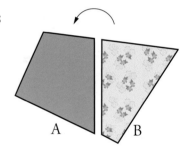

2. Allow top of B to extend ¼" over A.

3. Assembly-line sew all A/B pairs.

4. Clip connecting threads.

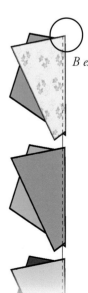

*B extends ¼".*

5.  Position pieces A/B with C. Flip C right sides together to A/B. Allow top of B to extend ¼".

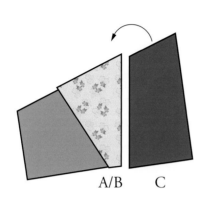

A/B     C

6.  Assembly-line sew.

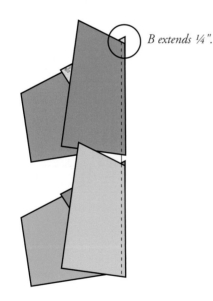

*B extends ¼".*

## Sewing Right Side Together

1.  Lay out stacks D and E. Flip E right sides together to D. Line up bottom of D and E.

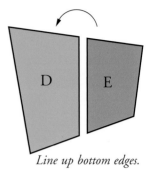

D    E

*Line up bottom edges.*

2.  Assembly-line sew.

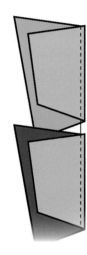

3.  Clip connecting threads.

4.  If you are going to embellish blocks with decorative stitching, press seams open. If you are not going to embellish blocks, press seams to one side.

5.  Sliver trim to straighten side of A/B/C and bottom edge on D/E.

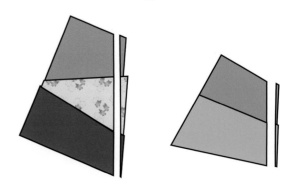

6.  Embellish seams with decorative stitches and contrasting thread, or topstitch lace on top of seams.

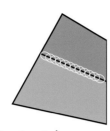

*Practice stitches on scraps before sewing them on pieces. If necessary, place tear away stabilizer under your stitches.*

7.  Lay out D/E pair with F. Flip F right sides together to D/E. Line up bottom edges. Assembly-line sew. Press seams.

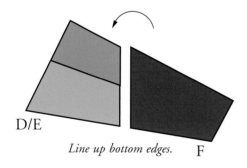

D/E

*Line up bottom edges.*    F

8.  Sliver trim to straighten edge on D/E/F.

9.  Embellish with decorative stitches or lace.

## Finishing Blocks

1.  Sew two halves together. Press seams.

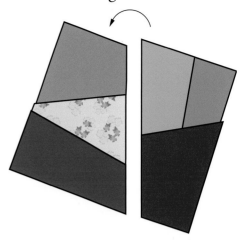

2.  Embellish new seams.

3.  Square each block to 5½".

*Center 6" Square Up Ruler on block. Straighten right and top side.*

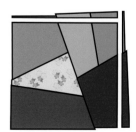

*Turn block and line up cut edges at 5½" on ruler. Straighten remaining two sides.*

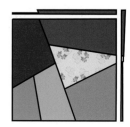

## Sewing Blocks Together

1. Arrange blocks in Stocking shape layout.

2. Sew blocks together.

3. Press seams.

## Quilting Stocking

1. Lay out batting. Center patchwork on top of batting, right side up.

2. Locate Stocking pattern on pattern sheet, and cut out.

3. Pin pattern to right side of patchwork.

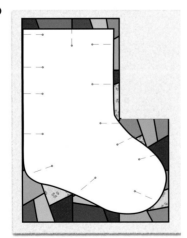

4. Cut out layers with scissors or rotary cutter.

5. Remove pattern. Pin layers together.

6. Embellish new seams through Stocking and batting.

## Completing Stocking

1. Lay out one back piece **wrong side up**.

2. Lay muslin lining, folded in half right sides together, on top of back.

3. Lay paper pattern on top. Pin.

4. Cut with scissors or rotary cutter.

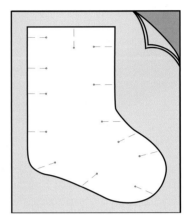

5. Lay out quilted Stocking, right side up. Place Stocking back right sides together to it. Lay both linings on top. Pin.

6. Sew around outside edge with generous ¼" seam. Leave top open. Clip curves.

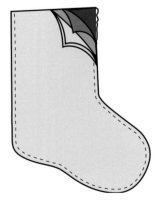

7. Reach between back and patchwork. Turn right side out. Check that all layers were sewn.

## Making Hanger

1. Fold 2" x 6" rectangle in half length-wise wrong sides together, and press.

2. Open and fold both edges to center crease. Press. Fold again. Press.

3. Sew ¼" in from edge.

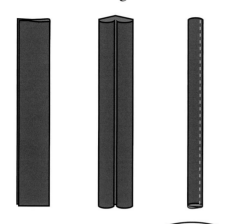

## Adding Cuff

1. Measure around opening of Stocking top. Add ½" to measurement for seam.

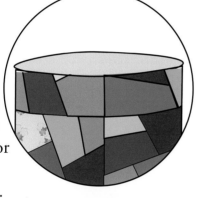

2. Cut 8" Cuff strip at that length.

3. Fold strip in half, right sides together. Sew ends together. Press seam open.

4. Turn right side out. Fold in half with raw edges together to form a circle. The seam is on the inside. If desired, embellish fold on Cuff with decorative stitches, lace, or name of receiver.

*Fold*

*Raw edges*

5. Pull two lining pieces apart. With raw edges up and seam to the left, tuck Cuff inside Stocking **between linings**. Match Cuff seam with Stocking seam. Place one pin at matched seam.

6. Tuck hanger between Cuff and lining to right of matched seam. Leave ends showing. Pin Cuff in place.

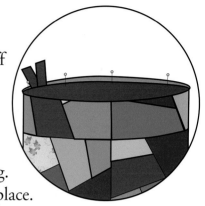

7. Sew with ¼" seam around top.

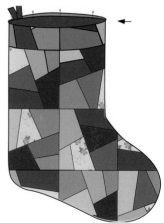

8. Pull Cuff out and fold down.

# Strip Stocking
## Eleanor Burns

## Supplies

Hand sewing needle

Template plastic

Ball point bodkin

Fat drinking straw

Permanent marking pen

Stiletto

## Yardage and Cutting

| Front | Assorted Prints |
|---|---|
| (12) 14" strips of assorted prints in a variety of widths from 1½" - 2¾" | |
| **Cuff** | **¼ yd** |
| (1) 8" x 20" strip<br>(1) 2" x 6" strip | |
| **Muslin Lining** | **½ yd** |
| (1) 16" x 42" | |
| **Back** | **½ yd** |
| (1) 16" x 21" | |
| **Thin Cotton Batting** | **16" x 21"** |
| **Green Holly** | **⅛ yd** |
| 4½" x 25" | |
| **Red Berries** | **⅛ yd** |
| (3) 2½" circles | |

*Fabrics used in this project are from Eleanor's Yours Truly Holiday line from Benartex.*

*14" x 17"*
*Find pattern in back of book.*

## Sewing Strips to Batting

1. Locate Stocking on pattern sheet, and cut out.

2. Place pattern on batting, and cut out one stocking.

3. Lay first strip right side up at an angle on batting. Allow extra fabric to hang over on both sides. Do not trim strip.

4. Place second strip right sides together to it. Allow extra strip to hang over on both sides. Stitch through all thicknesses. Unfold, and fingerpress.

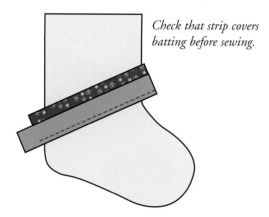

*Check that strip covers batting before sewing.*

5. Lay third strip right sides together to second strip. Stitch through all thicknesses. Unfold, and fingerpress.

6. Sew strips until batting stocking is covered to end of toe.

7. Turn, and continue sewing strips.

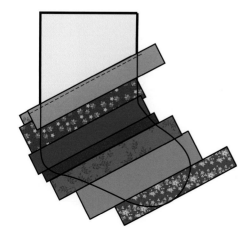

8. Cover batting stocking to top of Cuff.

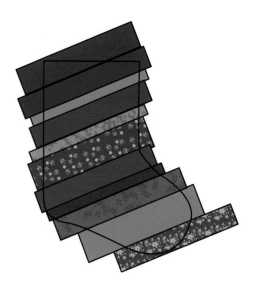

9. Trim away excess fabric from wrong side.

10. Turn to **Completing Stocking** on page 58.

# Making Holly

1. Trace Holly pattern from pattern sheet on template plastic, and cut out.

2. Fold 4½" x 25" green fabric right sides together.

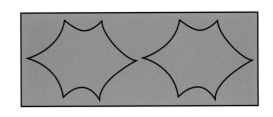

3. Trace two Holly on wrong side of fabric with permanent marking pen, leaving ½" space between the two.

4. Sew on lines with 20 stitches per inch or 1.8 on computerized machines.

5. Trim ⅛" away from stitching.

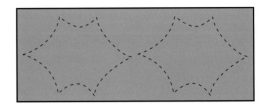

6. Clip small hole near top. Turn right side out with straw and ball point bodkin.

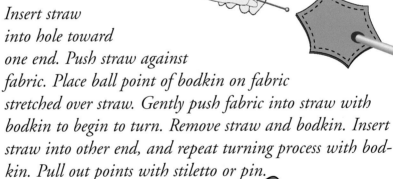

*Insert straw into hole toward one end. Push straw against fabric. Place ball point of bodkin on fabric stretched over straw. Gently push fabric into straw with bodkin to begin to turn. Remove straw and bodkin. Insert straw into other end, and repeat turning process with bodkin. Pull out points with stiletto or pin.*

7. Press Holly.

8. Hand stitch to top of Cuff.

## Making Berries

1. Find 2½" circle on pattern sheet. Trace circle on template plastic and cut out.

2. Trace three 2½" circles on red fabric, and cut out.

3. With hand sewing needle, run gathering stitch around outside edge of 2½" red fabric circles.

4. Lightly stuff with batting and draw up tightly.

5. Hand stitch Berries on top of Holly.

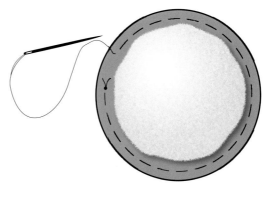

### Cheeseburger Soup

*from the kitchen of Eleanor Burns*

½ pound ground turkey
¾ cup chopped onion
¾ cup shredded carrots
¾ cup chopped celery
1 teaspoon dried basil
1 teaspoon dried parsley
4 tablespoons butter

1½ cups milk
3 cups chicken broth
4 cups cubed potatoes
½ cup all-purpose flour
2 cups cubed Cheddar cheese
1½ cups sour cream

In a large pot, cook and stir vegetables and turkey until turkey is brown. Drain fat. Stir in basil, parsley, broth, and potatoes. Bring to a boil, then simmer until potatoes are tender, about 10-12 minutes. In skillet, melt the butter and stir in flour. Add the milk, stirring until smooth. Gradually add milk mixture to the soup, stirring constantly. Bring to a boil and reduce heat to simmer. Stir in cheese. When cheese is melted, add sour cream and heat through. Do not boil.

# Bell and Santa Pillows
## Luckie Yasukochi

*18" x 18"*

*Find patterns in back of book.*

One 11 yd roll black
Clover Quick Bias® Tape
(fusible bias tape)

## Supplies

Black thread

Permanent marker

Soft lead pencil

Clover® Mini Iron (optional)

Marking pencils for both light and dark fabric

One 18" pillow form for each

## Bell Yardage

| Background | | ⅔ yd |
|---|---|---|
| (1) 20" square | | |
| **Pillow Back and Border** | | ½ yd |
| (2) 14" x 18½" pieces | | |
| (2) 1⅛" strips | | |
| **Applique Pieces** | | |
| Red Bow | 9" x 11" | |
| Gold Bell | 8" x 10" | |
| Gold Clapper | 2" x 5" | |
| **HeatnBond®** | | 1 yd |
| **Tear Away Stabilizer** | | ½ yd |
| **Thin Cotton Batting** | | 18" x 18" |

## Santa Yardage

| Background | | ⅔ yd |
|---|---|---|
| (1) 20" square | | |
| **Pillow Back and Border** | | ½ yd |
| (2) 14" x 18½" pieces | | |
| (2) 1⅛" strips | | |
| **Applique Pieces** | | |
| White Beard and Fur | 12½" x 12½" | |
| Red Hat | 6" x 12" | |
| Black Eyes | 2" x 5" | |
| Pink Face and Nose | 4" x 11" | |
| **HeatnBond®** | | 1 yd |
| **Tear Away Stabilizer** | | ½ yd |
| **Thin Cotton Batting** | | 18" x 18" |

## Tracing Placement Pattern onto Background

1. Place Placement Pattern right side up on table. Center 20" Background square right side up on pattern. If lines don't show through fabric, use a light box or your substitute.

2. With a soft lead pencil, lightly trace enough of pattern to show where to place pieces.

 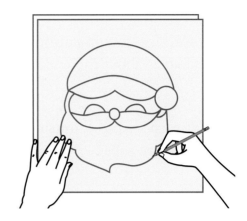

## Drawing Pattern Pieces

1. Lay Pattern sheet on table.

2. Place HeatnBond® on top, paper side up.

3. With permanent marker, trace all pattern shapes and lines. Notice pattern is mirror image of finished design.

 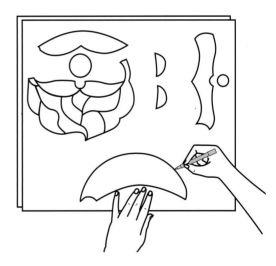

4. Rough cut shapes for each fabric. Do not remove paper back.

 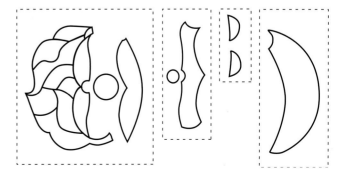

## Fusing Patterns to Fabric

1. Pair each pattern shape with its fabric.

2. Place fabric wrong side up on pressing mat. Lay fusible side of Heatnbond® against wrong side of fabric.

3. Use a hot, dry iron on cotton setting. Press all areas about three seconds.

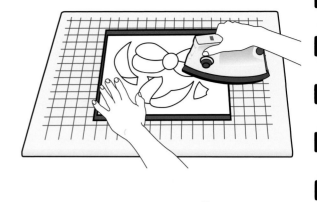

4. Cut out each shape on **outside line**. Do not remove paper.

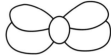

5. Using a light box or your substitute, place paper side against light. Draw lines for "inside" bias tape on right side of fabric.

## Appliqueing the Pieces

1. Remove paper from fused and marked pieces.

2. Place pieces on Background.

3. When satisfied with position, fuse each piece in place with hot, dry iron.

## Sewing Lead Lines

1. Place tear away stabilizer behind pillow front and pin in each corner.

2. Press Clover® Bias Tape over inside "lead" lines. Trim tape at start and finish points, following numbered order.

3. Press tape over outside lines to cover all raw edges.

4. Sew on both edges of bias tape with black thread.

*If necessary, lift tape with stiletto to tuck under raw edges.*

# Santa

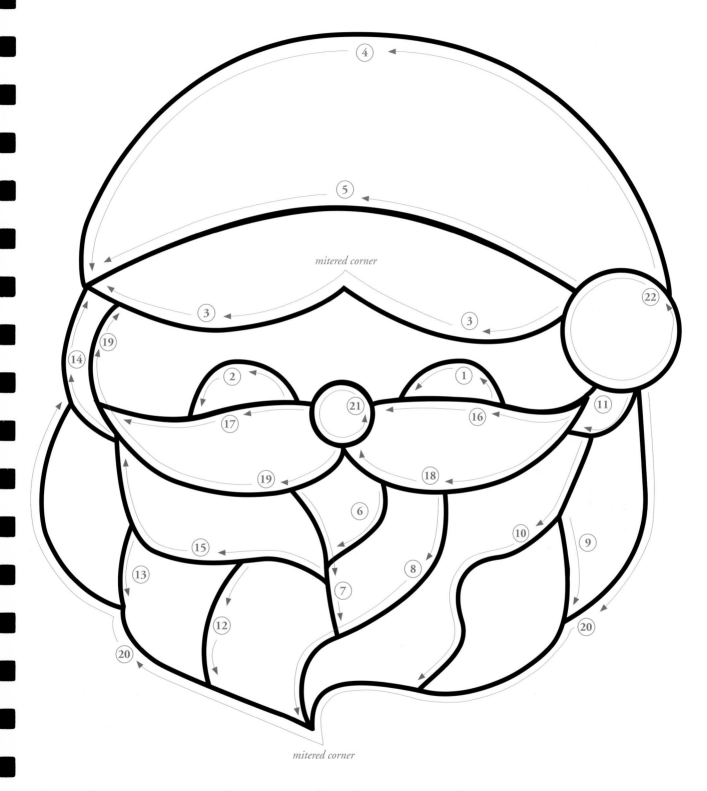

*mitered corner*

*mitered corner*

Cut and press bias tape in this order. Follow the direction of the arrows.

## Bell

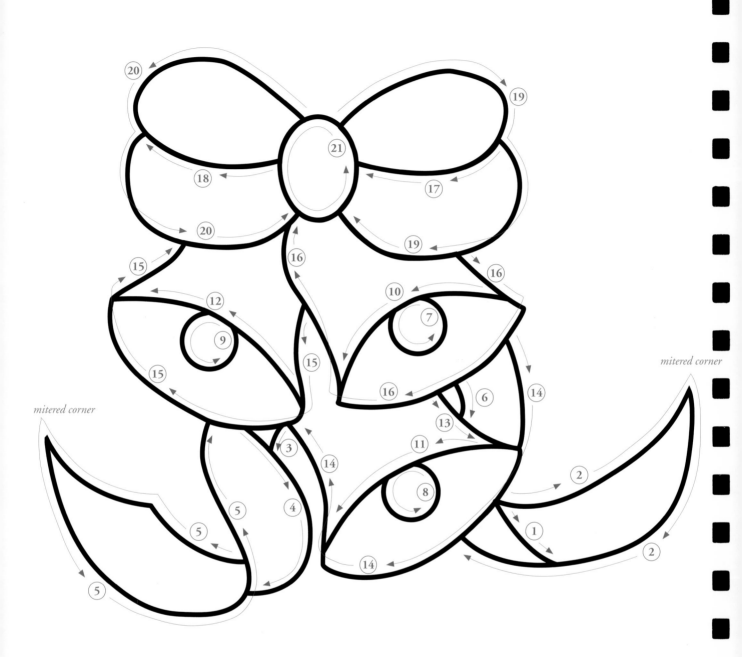

Cut and press bias tape in this order. Follow the direction of the arrows.

## Making the Pillow

1. Remove stabilizer from back of pillow front.

2. Press pillow front and trim to 16½" square.

3. Add 1⅛" Border on four sides.

4. Place pillow front on top of batting. Quilt through all layers ¼" from outside edge.

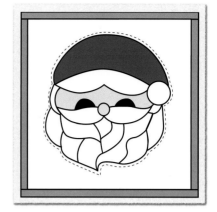

5. Select two 14" x 18½" pieces for back.

6. Along 14" side, fold under 2" twice. Do this for both pieces. Edge stitch.

7. Place pillow front right side up.

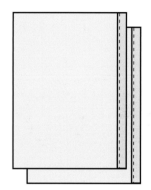

8. With folded edges facing up, place back pieces right sides together to front. Overlap two back pieces to make an 18½" square. Trim excess. Pin.

9. Sew around outside edge.

10. Turn right side out and insert pillow form.

*You can also turn Santa and Bell into wallhangings.*

# Teddy Bear
## Teresa Varnes

*Fabrics used in this Teddy Bear are from Eleanor's Yours Truly Holiday line from Benartex.*

## Yardage and Cutting

| | |
|---|---|
| Quilted fabric or chenille | 1 yd |
| 1½" wide Ribbon | 1 yd |
| or | |
| 3" wide Fabric strip | yd |
| Stuffing | 1 lb. bag |

## Supplies

Large scissors

Pins

Point turner

Permanent marking pen

(2) ½" buttons (optional)

*Give Teddy Bear a personality with chenille fabric.*

*18" tall*
*Find pattern in back of book.*

## Tips from Teresa

Cut out pieces with scissors.

Follow straight of grain.

Use ¼" seam allowance and 15 stitches per inch, or 2.0 on computerized machine.

Use needle down!

Pin or ease to fit parts together.

Backstitch on ends of seams so seams do not pull out while stuffing Bear.

Press seams in direction they lie the best.

Push out seams on turned pieces with point turner.

# Cutting Out Bear

1. Locate Teddy Bear pattern and cut out.

2. Fold fabric right sides together. Arrange and pin all pieces except front and back of Head. Pin front and back of Head on a single layer of fabric. Cut out shapes.

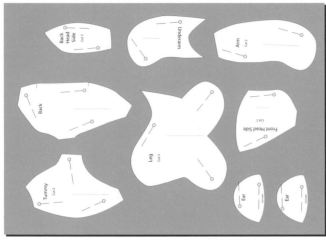

*Double layer of fabric*

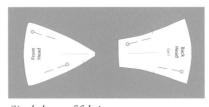

*Single layer of fabric*

3. Mark all notches with ⅛" scissor clip. Mark pivot points on wrong side of fabric pieces with dots from permanent marking pen.

4. Leave patterns attached to fabric pieces until they are used.

# Making Ears

1. With right sides together, sew Ears on curve.

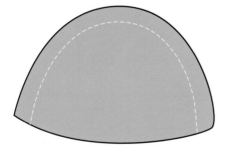

2. Fold together, matching seams.

3. Sew ½" tuck from both folded edges toward center.

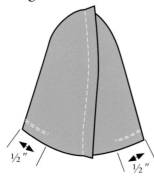

4. Turn right side out. Run point turner around inside curve. Push tuck seams in opposite directions.

5. Lightly stuff and baste raw edges closed.

# Making the Head

1. Lay out Front Head Center and Front Head Side pieces.

2. Flip right Front Head Side right sides together to Front Head Center piece. Start stitching from top.

3. Pin dot on Side to notch on Front.

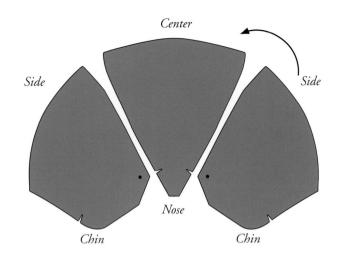

4. At notch, place needle down, raise presser foot and pivot. Continue to sew to end of Nose.

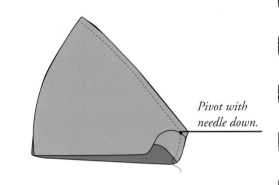

5. Open and flip Front Head Center over left Front Head Side. Pin and sew to notch, pivot, and sew to end of Nose.

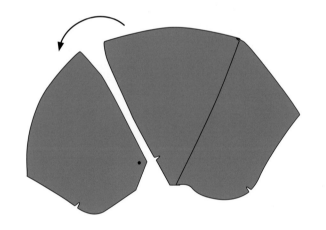

6. Turn wrong side out. Match up raw edges for Chin. Sew from end of Nose to notch at end of Chin. Turn right side out.

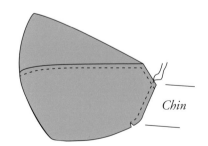

7.  Line up tucks on Ears with seams on Head, and pin. Baste Ears to Head with scant ¼" seam.

8.  Lay out Back Head Center and Back Head Side pieces.

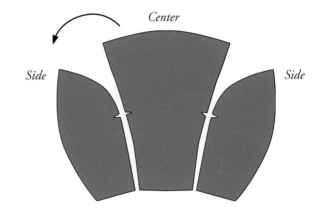

9.  Flip Back Head Center right sides together to left Back Head Side piece. Start stitching from the top, match notches, and stitch to bottom.

10. Open and flip right Back Head Side over Back Head Center. Start stitching from the top, match notches, and stitch to bottom.

11. With right sides together, pin front of Head to back of Head. Sew together. Turn right sides out. Check to make sure Ears are properly attached.

## Making Legs

1. Fold and pin Leg pieces right sides together.

2. Stitch, pivoting and reinforcing the point where Leg and Feet meet.

3. Clip reinforced seam.

4. Turn right side out.

*Be careful to sew mirror image Legs.*

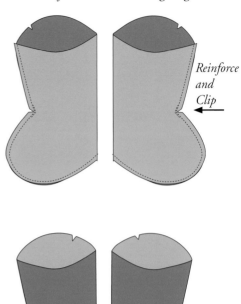

*Reinforce and Clip*

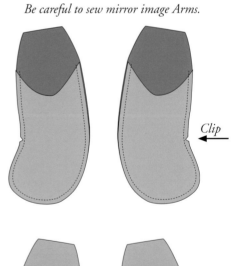

## Making Arms

1. Match and pin Underarm to Arm, right sides together.

2. Sew around Arm, and clip.

3. Turn right side out.

*Be careful to sew mirror image Arms.*

*Clip*

## Making Body

1. Sew center front seam on Tummy, right sides together.

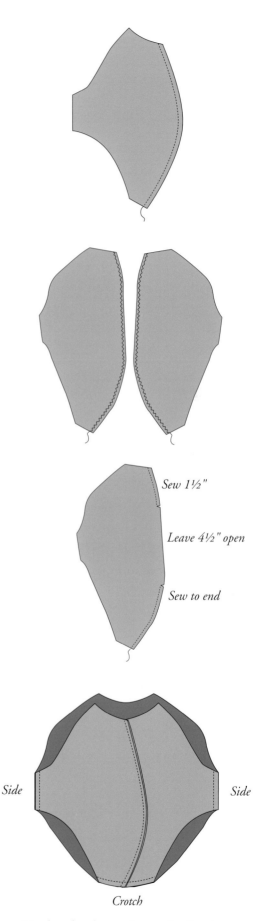

2. On Back pieces, staystitch with ¼" zig-zag stitch.

3. Place Back pieces right sides together. Sew center Back seam 1½" and stop. Leave 4½" opening for stuffing Bear. Continue sewing back seam.

*Sew 1½"*

*Leave 4½" open*

*Sew to end*

4. Place Tummy and Back right sides together, and pin. Sew crotch and side seams.

5. Do not turn right side out.

*Side*　　　　　　　　　　　　　　*Side*

*Crotch*

*Match and push seams in opposite directions.*

# Finishing Bear

1. Place Body with Tummy side up. Place Legs with toes pointing up toward Tummy.

2. Insert Legs into Body, toes first.

3. Match notch on Leg to side seam on Body, right sides together, and pin. Sew with Leg on top. Continue with other Leg. *This technique is similar to sewing a hem on a cuff.*

4. Turn Body right side out.

5. With right sides together, pin left Arm to Body at front of Bear. Begin sewing at **front** of Bear, pull Arm to Body, matching an inch at a time, and sew. *This technique is similar to sewing a crotch on a pair of pants.*

6. With right sides together, pin right Arm to Body at back of Bear. Pull Arm to Body, matching an inch at a time, and sew.

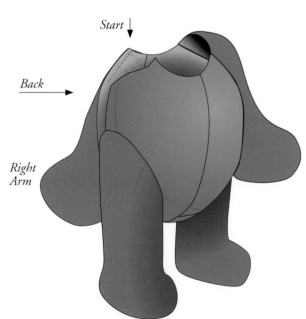

7. Turn Body wrong side out through neck hole.

8. Tuck Head inside Body, Ears first and Nose pointing toward Tummy, so fabrics are right sides together.

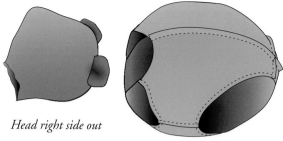

*Head right side out*

*Body wrong side out*

9. Match and pin front Head seam with center Body seam. Sew neck seam with Head side up.

10. Turn right side out through stuffing hole in back.

11. Firmly stuff Legs, then Arms, then Head, and finish with Body.

12. Hand stitch opening on Back.

13. For Fabric Bow, cut ends of 3" strip on diagonal, or use ribbon.

14. Tie Bow around Bear's neck.

15. Sew on optional buttons for Eyes.

# Country Table Setting

Page 90

# Any Season Tablerunner and Lone Pine Placemats

**Sandy Thompson**

*When we were kids, my sisters, my mom and I always made cookies for Christmas. My favorite cookie is Grandma's Cut Out Sugar Cookie. Each year we made dozens and dozens of these cut out cookies. Then, as a family we all got together and had a wonderful contest seeing who could decorate their cookie the best.*

*Today, I carry on the tradition by baking these cookies with a few minor changes. I don't use the frosting and I cut them out with my dog bone cookie cutter. Then, my dog Billy and I deliver them to our family veterinarian.*

*Cookie recipe on page 93.*

Page 80

# Any Season Tablerunner
## Sandy Thompson

## Yardage and Cutting

| Background | 1 yd |
|---|---|

- (3) 9" squares
- (2) 8" squares
- (1) 7½" square
- (1) 2¾" x 40" strip cut into
    - (2) 2¾" x 20"
- (4) 3½" squares
- (2) 2" x 6½"

| Print | ¾ yd |
|---|---|

Border
- (4) 3½" strips

Four-Patches
- (2) 2½" x 25" strips

Star Center
- (1) 4" x 8"

| Trees | ¼ yd of three greens |
|---|---|

- (1) 7½" square from each

| Star Center and Four-Patches | ¼ yd green |
|---|---|

Star Center
- (1) 4" x 8"

Four-Patches
- (2) 2½" x 25" strips

| Star Points and Pinwheels | ⅓ yd of two reds |
|---|---|

Star Points
- (1) 9" square from one

Four Pinwheel Blocks
- (1) 8" square from both

| Trunks | ⅛ yd |
|---|---|

- (1) 2⅛" x 20"

| Backing | 1 yd |
|---|---|

| Binding | ½ yd |
|---|---|

- (5) 3" strips

| Batting | 22" x 74" |
|---|---|

*17½" x 67½"*

## Supplies

3" x 6" Flying Geese Ruler

6½" Triangle Square Up Ruler

## Making Four-Patches

1. Sew 2½" print and 2½" green strips right sides together. Make two sets.

2. Set seams, open, and press to green.

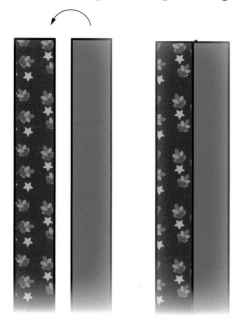

3. Place first strip right side up on cutting mat with print across top. Layer second strip right sides together to it with green across top. Lock seams. Line up strips with lines on cutting mat, or use Shape Cut.

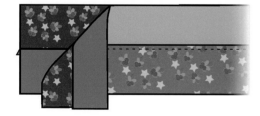

4. Square left end. Cut nine 2½" pairs.

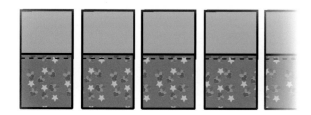

5. Separate three pairs and sew end to end. Make two sets.

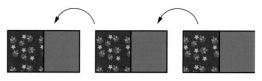

6. Press seams in same direction.

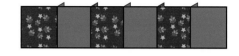

7. Sew remaining six pairs into Four-Patches.

8. Lay Four-Patch on table, wrong side up. Finger press top center seam to right, and bottom center seam to left. Center stitches will pop open.

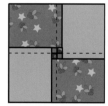

9. Press little center Four-patch open and flat.

10. Sew three Four-Patches together. Make two sets.

11. Press new seams in same direction.

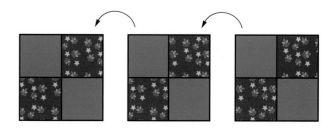

81

## Making Star Center

1. Place 4" x 8" green and 4" x 8" print right sides together.

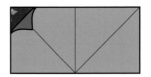

2. Draw center line at 4", and one diagonal line in each square.

3. Sew ¼" from both sides of diagonal lines. Set seams.

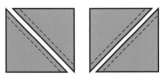

4. Cut apart on all drawn lines.

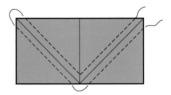

5. Square patches to 3½" with Triangle Square Up Ruler. Trim tips. Press seams toward green fabric.

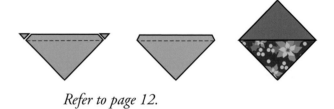

*Refer to page 12.*

6. Lay out patches to form Star Center. Assembly-line sew.

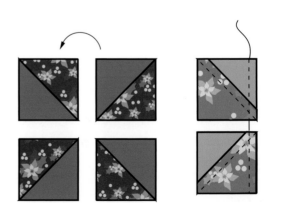

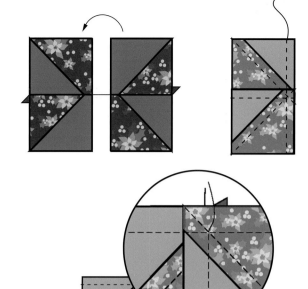

7. Open, and flip right sides together. Lock top seam up and underneath seam down, and sew.

8. At center seam, cut first stitch with scissors.

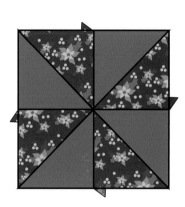

9. Lay block on table wrong side up. Finger press top center seam to right, and bottom center seam to left. Center stitches will pop open.

10. Press little pinwheel open and flat.

11. Center should measure 6½" square.

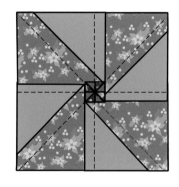

## Making Points for Star

1. Place one 7½" Background square right sides together and centered on one 9" red square.

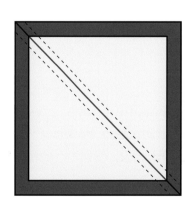

2. Make one set of dark Star Points following instructions beginning on page 18.

3. Square up to 3½" x 6½" using green 3" x 6" markings on Flying Geese Ruler.

# Finishing Star

1. Lay out Star Center with 3½" x 6½" Star Points and four 3½" Background squares.

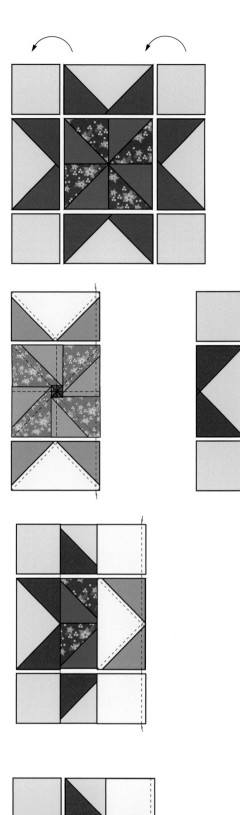

2. Flip middle vertical row to left vertical row. Assembly-line sew vertical seam.

3. Open and add right vertical row.

4. Sew remaining rows, pressing seams away from Star Points.

5. Press.

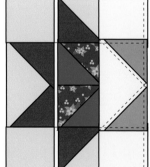

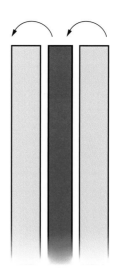

## Making Tree Trunks

1. Sew 2¾" x 20" Background strips to 2⅛" x 20" Trunk strip.

2. Set seams, open, and press toward Trunk.

3. Cut into two 3½" pieces and six 2" pieces.

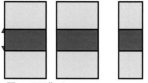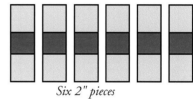

*Two 3½" pieces*  *Six 2" pieces*

## Making Trees

1. Place three different 7½" green squares right sides together and centered on three 9" Background squares.

2. Make three sets of Flying Geese from each of the three different greens following instructions beginning on page 14.

3. Square to 3½" x 6½" using green 3" x 6" markings on Flying Geese Ruler.

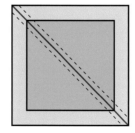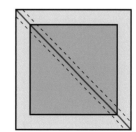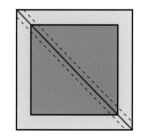

4. Stack into three piles with same green in each pile.

5. Sew four pairs together. Leave four single.

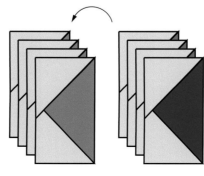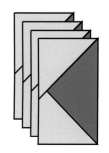

6.  Sew 3½" Trunks to bottoms of
    two tall Trees.

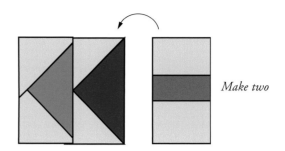

*Make two*

7.  Sew 2" Trunks to bottoms of four single Trees.

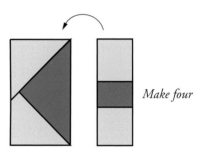

*Make four*

8.  Sew 2" Trunks to bottoms of two Trees.

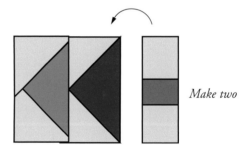

*Make two*

9.  Sew 2" x 6½" Background to tops of
    two Trees with 2" Trunks.

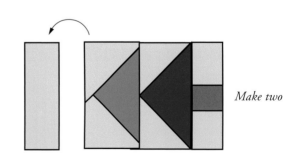

*Make two*

10. Sew Trees together. Make two sets.

11. Press seams down toward Trunks.

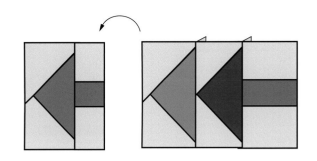

12. Sew Trees together. Make two sets.

13. Press seams up from Trunks.

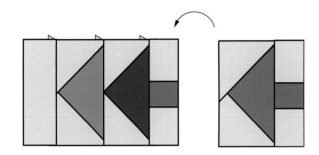

14. Lay out two different sets of Trees. Match and lock seams. Sew together.

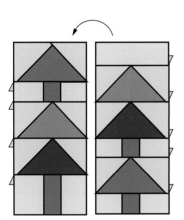

15. Press final seam to right.

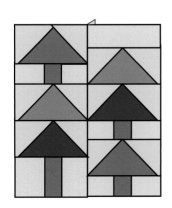

## Making Four Pinwheels

1. Place an 8" Background square right sides together to each red square.

2. Draw diagonal lines on wrong side of Background squares.

3. Sew exactly ¼" from lines. Press to set seams.

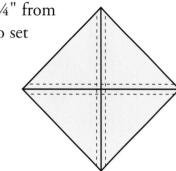

4. Without moving fabric, cut squares horizontally and vertically.

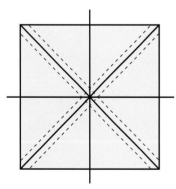

5. Cut on both diagonal lines.

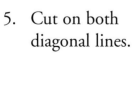

6. Square to 3½" with Triangle Square Up Ruler. Trim tips. Press seams to red.

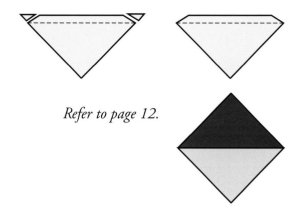

*Refer to page 12.*

7. Sew four Pinwheel blocks together. Follow instructions from Star Center, pages 82-83, steps #6 - #11.

8. Sew two sets of pinwheels together for runner ends.

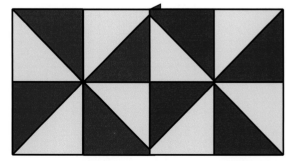

9. From right side, press final seam to right.

## Sewing Tablerunner Together

1. Lay out blocks and sew together.

2. Press seams toward Four-Patch rows.

3. Add 3½" Borders.

4. Turn to **Finishing Your Quilt** on page 196.

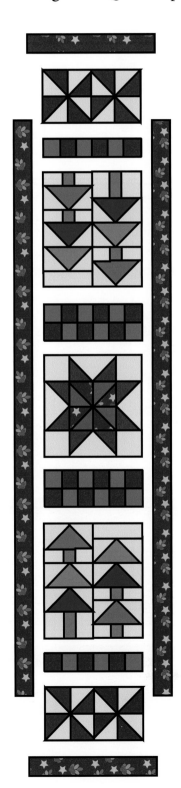

*If you wish to use your project as a long narrow wallhanging, turn both Tree sections in the same direction.*

# Lone Pine Placemats
## Sandy Thompson

*14" x 18"*

## Yardage and Cutting for Four Placemats

| Print | ¾ yd |
|---|---|

Border
- (2) 2½" strips cut into
  - (4) 2½" x 10½"
- (4) 2½" strips cut into
  - (8) 2½" half strips

Four-Patches
- (2) 2½" strips cut into
  - (2) 2½" x 30"

| Background | ¾ yd |
|---|---|

Center
- (1) 10½" strip cut into
  - (4) 10½" x 9½"

Trees
- (4) 6" squares
- (2) 1¾" x 20"

| Four Greens | ¼ yd of each |
|---|---|

Trees
- (1) 4½" square from each green

Four-Patches from one green
- (2) 2½" x 30"

| Trunk | ⅛ yd |
|---|---|

- (1) 1⅛" x 20"

| Binding | ¾ yd |
|---|---|

- (8) 3" strips

| Backing | 1 yd |
|---|---|

| Batting | 36" x 45" |
|---|---|

## Supplies

3" x 6" Flying Geese Ruler with 1½" x 3" markings

# Making Four-Patches

1. Sew 2½" x 30" print and 2½" x 30" green right sides together. Make two sets.

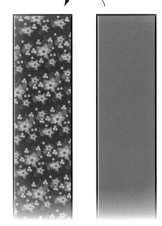

2. Set seams, open, and press to green.

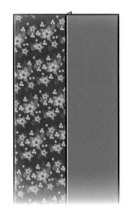

3. Place first strip right side up on cutting mat with print across top. Layer second strip right sides together to it with green across top. Lock seams. Line up strips with lines on cutting mat.

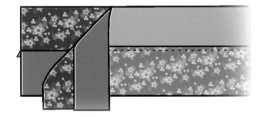

4. Square left end. Cut ten 2½" pairs.

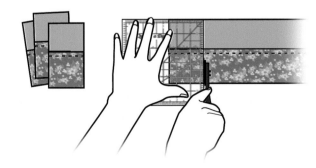

5. Separate two pairs into four singles and set aside.

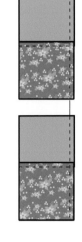

6. Sew remaining eight pairs into Four-Patches.

7. Open center seam. See page 81, step #8.

8. Sew together two Four-Patches. Make four sets.

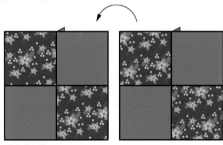

*Make four sets.*

9. Sew one single unit to each Four-Patch.

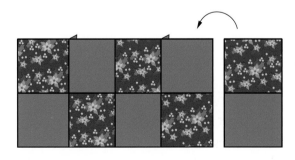

10. Measure. Four-Patches should be 10½" long.

## Making Tree Trunks

1. Sew 1¾" Background strip to 1⅛" Trunk strip.

2. Set seams, open, and press toward Trunk.

3. Sew 1¾" Background strip to other side of Trunk strip.

4. Set seams, open, and press toward Trunk.

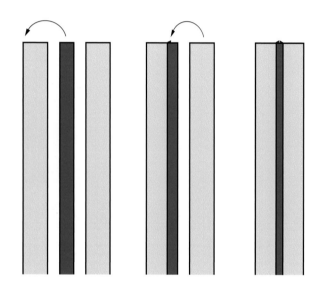

5. Cut into four 4½" pieces.

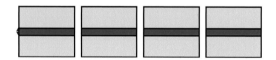

## Making Trees

1. Place four different 4½" green squares right sides together and centered on four 6" Background squares.

2. Make Flying Geese following instructions beginning on page 14.

3. Square to 2" x 3½" using red 1½" x 3" markings on 3" x 6" Flying Geese ruler.

4. Stack into four piles with same green in each pile.

5. Sew together into pairs.

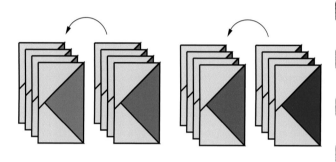

6. Sew pairs together.

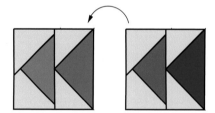

7. Sew a Trunk to bottom of each Tree.

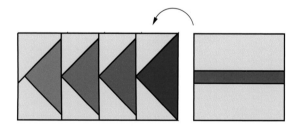

8. Press all seams from Trunk to top of Tree.

9. Measure. Tree unit should be 10½" long.

# Finishing Placemats

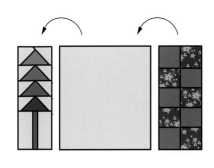

1. Sew Tree to left side of 10½" x 9½" Background Center.

2. Sew Four-Patches to right side of Background Center.

3. Sew 2½" x 10½" Border to left side of Trees.

4. Press seams away from Tree and Four-Patches.

5. Sew 2½" Border half strips to top and bottom.

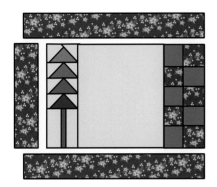

6. Press seams toward Border. Trim if necessary.

7. Turn to **Finishing Your Quilt** on page 196.

---

### Grandma's Cut Out Sugar Cookies

*from the kitchen of Sandy Thompson*

1 cup butter
1½ cups sugar
1¼ teaspoons salt
2 teaspoons vanilla

2 teaspoons almond extract
2 eggs
2½ cups flour

Mix all ingredients except flour until smooth. Mix in flour. Refrigerate at least one hour. Roll to ¼" and cut out cookies. Bake at 375° for 8-10 minutes.

**Icing (makes 2 cups)**
3 large egg whites
1 (16 oz.) package powdered sugar

½ teaspoon cream of tartar
*Optional:* Food Coloring

Combine egg whites and cream of tartar in large bowl and beat until stiff. Gradually add powdered sugar.

*Note:* Icing dries quickly; keep bowl covered with a damp towel.

# Victorian Tea Time

Melissa Varnes

## Tea Cups

*We are accustomed to celebrating the Feast of Epiphany on January sixth. It is part of my mom's background in the Mexican culture, known as The Three Kings Day, or El Dia del los Tres Reyes. It observes the coming of the wise men bringing gifts to the Christ child, which is the day that "reveals" Jesus to the world as Lord and King.*

*Every year, on the eve of Epiphany, my sister and I leave our shoes outside our door. The following morning, we wake to find gifts left on our shoes that The Three Kings brought us.*

Page 104

94

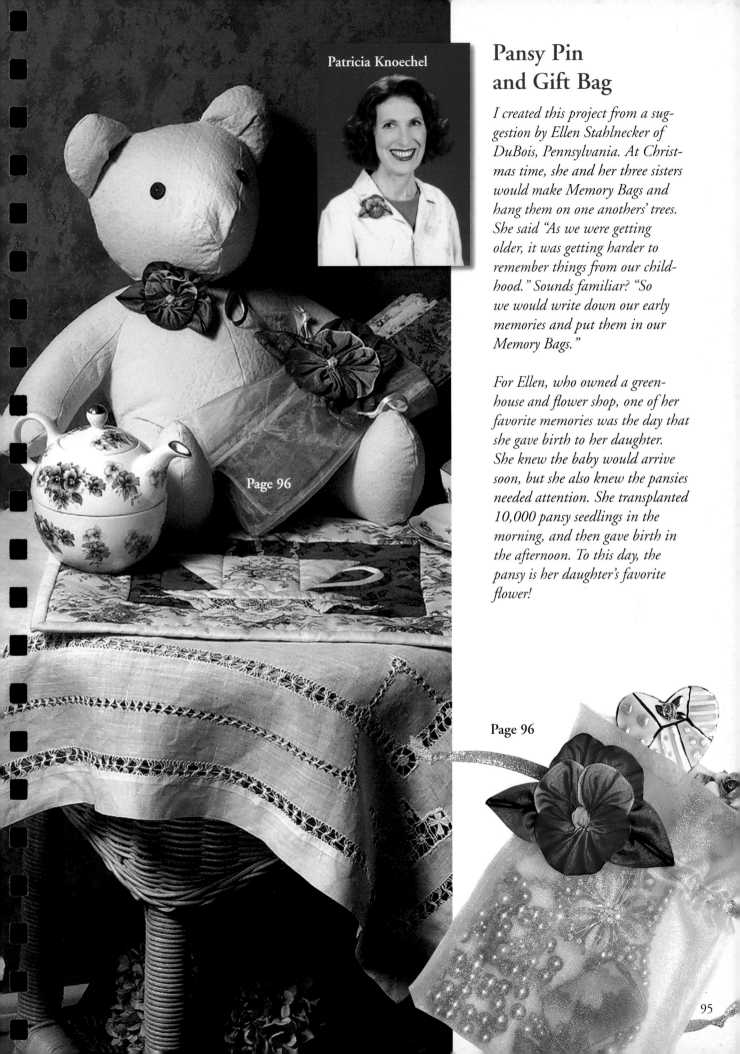

**Patricia Knoechel**

# Pansy Pin and Gift Bag

*I created this project from a suggestion by Ellen Stahlnecker of DuBois, Pennsylvania. At Christmas time, she and her three sisters would make Memory Bags and hang them on one anothers' trees. She said "As we were getting older, it was getting harder to remember things from our childhood." Sounds familiar? "So we would write down our early memories and put them in our Memory Bags."*

*For Ellen, who owned a greenhouse and flower shop, one of her favorite memories was the day that she gave birth to her daughter. She knew the baby would arrive soon, but she also knew the pansies needed attention. She transplanted 10,000 pansy seedlings in the morning, and then gave birth in the afternoon. To this day, the pansy is her daughter's favorite flower!*

**Page 96**

**Page 96**

95

# Pansy Pin and Gift Bag
## Patricia Knoechel

*Select variegated or Ombre wire edge ribbon for your pansies. Directions are given for two sizes of pansies, depending on width and length of wire ribbon. Select organdy or any luxurious fabric for your Gift Bag.*

*The smaller pansy from ⅞" wire ribbon makes a nice pin and fits on the Gift Bag. The larger pansy from 1½" wide wire ribbon looks nice as an embellishment on a gift.*

*Small Pansy 3½"*
*Large Pansy 5½"*

## Yardage and Cutting

### Small Pansy

Pansy
> ½ yd of ⅞" wide ribbon cut into
> > (1) 10½"
> > (2) 3½"

Leaves
> 6" of 1½" wide green ribbon cut into
> > (2) 1½" x 3"

### Large Pansy

Pansy
> 1 yd of 1½" wide ribbon cut into
> > (1) 18"
> > (2) 6"

Leaves
> (1) 5½" circle green fabric

### Center Options for Both Pansies

Center
> 5" of ¾" to 1" wide yellow ribbon or 1-3 beads

### Crinoline

> 2" square

*stiff net-like material used as base on which petals are sewn*

### Gift Bag          ¼ yd

> (1) 6" x 18"

> (2) 18" lengths ¼" wide ribbon

*5½" x 6"*

## Supplies

Strong thread as Quilting thread, Buttonhole Twist, or double strand of regular thread

Hand sewing needle

Beading needle (optional)

Ball point bodkin

Fray Check™

## Making Back Petals

1. Thread needle with double strand of regular matching thread, or single strand of heavy thread. Knot on end.

2. Overlap two lengths of ribbon perpendicular to one another. Position with the **darker value along top edge.**

3. Place a pin diagonally at center.

4. Begin stitching on right side. *Left hand sewers start on left side.* Back stitch over knot by wrapping thread around edge of ribbon. Tug to assure a tight knot. Take long stitches.

*Small Pansy (2) 3½" lengths*

*Large Pansy (2) 6" lengths*

5. Draw in gathers to form two petals. Tie a knot at end but do not clip thread.

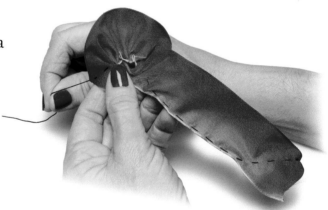

6. Tack petals to upper half of crinoline. Stitch close to gathers, in the folds. Cut thread.

## Making Three Front Petals

1. Thread needle with matching thread. Knot on end.

2. Lay out variegated ribbon horizontally with **lighter value along top edge**.

3. Divide ribbon into three equal sections and place pins along bottom edge. Pin Small Pansy every 3½", or Large Pansy every 6".

*Small Pansy (1) 10½" length   Large Pansy (1) 18" length*

4. Turn under each side at pin.

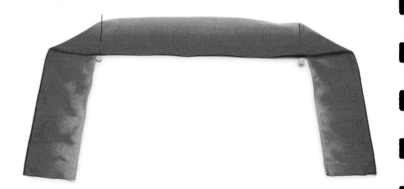

5. Reposition pins on diagonal folds. Beginning on right side, back stitch, then stitch with ¼" long stitches.

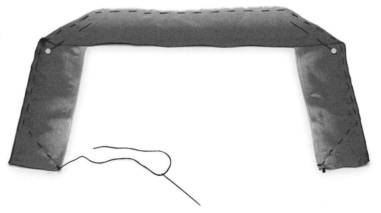

6. Gather tightly to form three petals with a small opening in center.

7. Tie a knot at the end, but do not cut thread until center is in place.

## Sewing Beads to Center Option

1. Connect petals and knot.

2. Add beads with beading needle.

3. Cut thread.

## Making Center from Yellow Ribbon Option

1. Tie a knot in middle of yellow ribbon. Position knot in center opening of three petals.

2. With attached thread, join two center petals, tightly closing opening over yellow ribbon.

3. Trim ends of yellow ribbon to ½".

## Finishing Pansy

1. Tack three petals onto crinoline below back petals.

2. Hide stitches in folds of gathers. Trim crinoline.

3. Cut thread.

## Making Small Pansy Leaves

1. Thread needle with matching thread. Knot on end.

2. Position 1½" x 3" green variegated ribbon with **dark value along top edge**. Fold in half and mark center with pin.

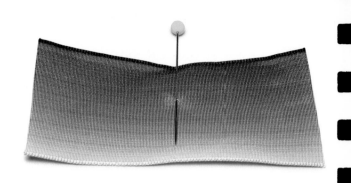

3. At center, fold sides down on diagonal.

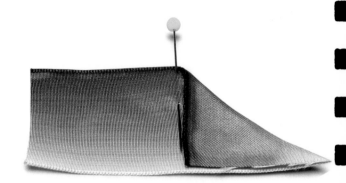

4. Stitch along bottom edge and gather loosely.

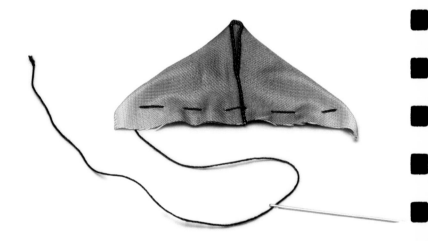

5. Tie knot but do not clip thread.

6. Tuck leaves under flower petals and tack to crinoline.

Optional: Sew or glue pin back to Pansy and wear as a pin. Use to decorate Gift Bag.

## Making Large Pansy Leaves

1. Cut 5½" circle in half.

2. Fold in half right sides together, and sew ¼" seam.

3. Fold so seam runs down center.

4. Thread needle with double strand of matching thread. Knot on end.

5. Stitch along bottom edge and gather loosely.

6. Tie knot but do not clip thread.

7. Tuck leaves under flower petals and tack to crinoline.

Optional: Use to decorate a gift.

## Making Gift Bag

5½" x 6" finished size

1. Fold 6" x 18" fabric in half length wise. If your fabric has a right side, fold right side together.

2. With matching thread, backstitch, and stitch ¼" along right side only.

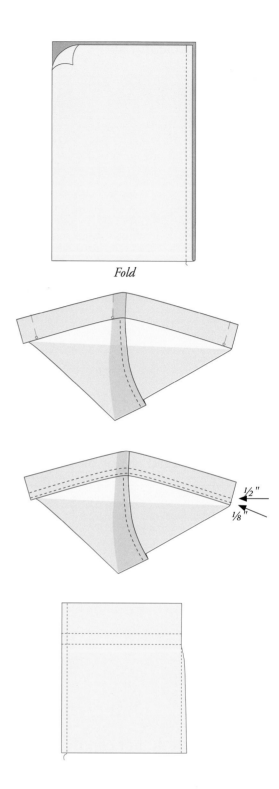

*Fold*

3. Measure 2" down from top edge and turn over to wrong side.

4. Pin in place at each side and in center.

5. To make casing, stitch ⅛" from bottom edge, and again ½" up from stitches.

½"

⅛"

6. Stitch ¼" seam on remaining side. Turn right side out.

7. With sharp scissors, cut small slits in casing on both sides of both seams.

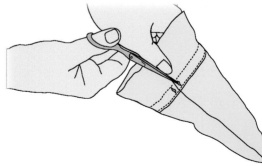

8. Trim end of an 18" length of ribbon at an angle. Thread through hole in ball point bodkin.

9. Insert ball point of bodkin into a slit in casing.

10. Pull ribbon through casing and out opposite side. Loop around and continue through casing on opposite side of bag.

11. Pull ribbon so that both ends extend evenly.

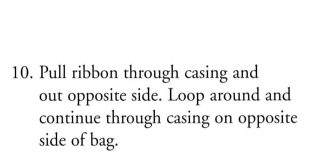

12. With second ribbon, begin on opposite side and repeat.

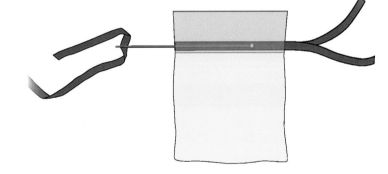

13. Hold two ends together and tie a knot about 2½" from the bag. Trim ends and apply Fray Check™.

14. Repeat on opposite side

# Tea Cups Melissa Varnes

*11½" x 14"*

*14" x 29"*

## Supplies

Permanent marking pen

Template plastic

40" String

## Yardage and Cutting for Four Tea Cups

| Background | ⅜ yd |
|---|---|

Cup
- (2) 3" strips cut into
  - (2) 3" x 6" pairs
  - (4) 2½" x 5½"
- (3) 1½" strips cut into
  - (8) 1½" x 10"
  - (4) 1½" x 5½"
  - (8) 1½" squares

| Lattice, Border and Binding | ⅔ yd |
|---|---|

- (8) 2½" strips

| Tea Cup | ½ yd |
|---|---|

Cups
- (2) 3" strips cut into
  - (2) 3" x 6" pairs
  - (5) 3" x 4½" (one for tea bag pocket)

Handle
- (1) 6" strip

Saucer
- (1) 1½" strip cut into
  - (4) 1½" x 7"

**One or two 6" doilies cut in half**

| Backing | ½ yd |
|---|---|

| Batting | 18" x 45" |
|---|---|

## Making Sides of Tea Cup

1. Lay out pairs of 3" x 6" rectangles **wrong sides together** in both Background and Tea Cup fabrics. Layer cut on one diagonal.

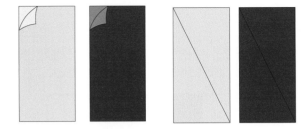

2. Stack Background and Tea Cup triangles right side up. Place four in each stack. The sets are mirror image of each other.

3. Flip right sides together.

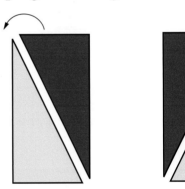

*The sets are mirror image of each other.*

4. **Extend ⅜" tip at both ends.** Assembly-line sew.

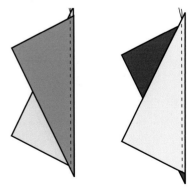

5. Set seams with Tea Cup on top, open, and press toward Tea Cup.

## Squaring Sides

1. Cut 2½" x 4½" rectangle from template plastic.

2. Place rectangle on pattern and trace diagonal line. Note diagonal line is ⅛" in from both corners. Find patterns on page 109.

3. Lay out left and right sides of Tea Cup.

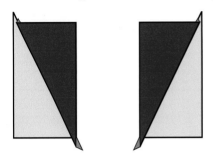

4. Place template on left patch. Trace around template. Cut on lines.

5. Flip template over. Place template on right patch. Trace around template.

6. Cut on lines.

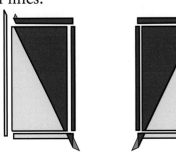

## Making Optional Pocket for Tea Bag

1. On one 3" side of 3" x 4½" rectangle, fold ⅜" under twice and press. Edgestitch.

2. Place Pocket right side up on top of second 3" x 4½" rectangle. Baste sides with ⅛" seam.

### Finishing Middle of Cup

1. Lay out three pieces, and sew together.

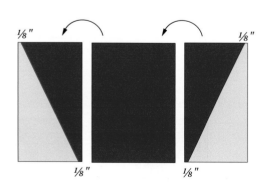

2. Press seams toward center.

## Adding Saucer

1. Draw diagonal lines on wrong side of 1½" Background squares.

2. Place 1½" squares right sides together to ends of 1½" x 7" Saucer strip.

3. Sew on diagonal lines. Trim ¼" away.

4. Set seams, open, and press toward Background.

5. Sew Saucer to Cup.

6. Press seam toward Saucer.

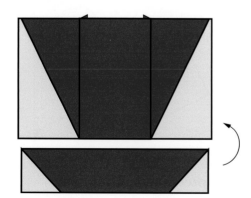

## Making Handle

7. Sew Background strips to sides. Set seams, open, and press toward Background.

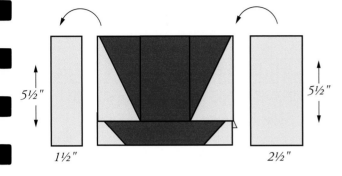

5½"

1½"

5½"

2½"

1. Make Handle template. Center template on side of Cup, and trace around template.

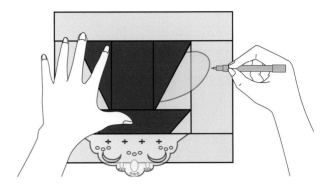

8. Cut doily in half. Center and baste to bottom of Cup.

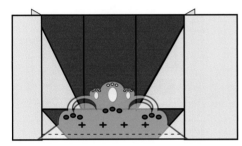

2. From corner of 6" strip, cut 1¼" x 7½" strip on bias for each Cup.

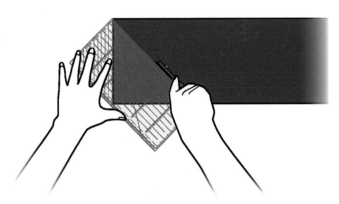

9. Sew Background strips to top and bottom. Set seams, open, and press toward Saucer.

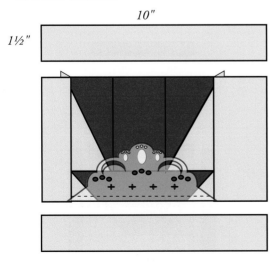

10"

1½"

3. Tie knot on end of 10" piece of string.

4. Lay string on right side of 1¼" x 7½" bias strip. Extend knot.

5. Fold strip right sides together, and sew across top and down right side. Trim seam to ⅛".

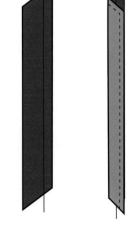

6. Pull on string and turn bias strip right side out. Cut string.

7. Press.

8. Pin bias strip on traced line, extending 1" at beginning and end.

9. Unsew stitches for two openings in side seam of Cup. Tuck ends of Handle into openings.

10. Handstitch Handle and two openings.

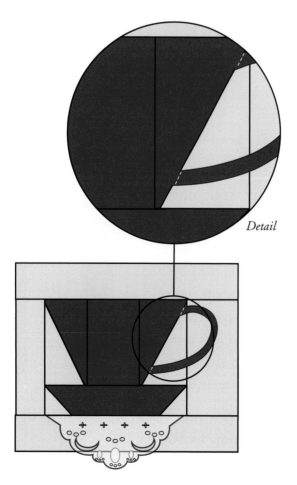

*Detail*

## Finishing

1. Measure width of Tea Cups, approximately 10".

2. Cut four 2½" Lattice strips to that measurement for the Three Cup and two 2½" Lattice for the One Cup.

3. Lay out Lattice and Side Borders.

4. Sew Lattice with Tea Cups. Add Side Borders.

5. Turn to **Finishing Your Quilt** on page 196.

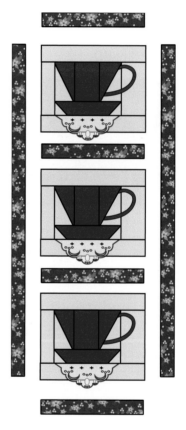

*Sides Template*

*Handle Template*

*I wish we could
sit down together and
drink a cup of tea.
But since we can't,
when you have this...
I hope you'll think of me!*

## Flan

*from the kitchen of Teresa Varnes*

⅓ cup sugar
1 (14 oz.) can sweetened condensed milk
2 teaspoons vanilla
2 tablespoons Kahlua *(optional)*

5 eggs
1 can evaporated milk
1 (8 oz.) package cream cheese

Place sugar in aluminum loaf pan. Hold loaf pan over low heat, moving pan from side to side until sugar is completely melted and golden brown. Swirl to coat sides and bottom evenly with the sugar. Set aside.

Beat eggs and cream cheese well. Add sweetened condensed milk and evaporated milk and beat until blended. Beat in vanilla. Add optional Kahlua if desired. Pour mixture into aluminum loaf pan and place in a larger pan containing 1" hot water. Bake at 350° 1 hour, or until toothpick inserted in center comes out clean. Cool; then turn over on a serving plate.

# Small Wallhangings

Eleanor Burns

Page 112

## Bear's Paw Christmas

*I love to light tons of candles and oil
lamps for Christmas dinner. For extra
warmth, I clip single candles to each
person's dinner plate. Family tradition
is for each to tell what they are thank-
ful for before blowing out their candle.
The plan is to have them burn the whole
dinner, but once my sons eagerly start
passing serving dishing around, they
have to dodge their plate candles. Now,
the smart ones tell what they are thank-
ful for as soon as they sit down, so they
can quickly blow out their candle!*

## Cold Hands, Warm Heart

*As the rest of us get older, we realize that the greatest gift is in sharing the joy of being together. My mother, who we all call Oma, is now 81 years young. She still takes the time to shop and prepare the Dutch goodies we all associate with our holiday, and spends days creating the "Chocolate Letters" which are a sweet symbol of her devotion for all of us.*

**Page 126**

Anne Dease

Marie Harper

## Mortimer Moose Wallhanging

*On Christmas Eve, with Santa's visit close, it is difficult putting excited children to bed. The tradition in my dad's family was to have a gift tucked under the pillow. When we were in bed and intended to STAY there, we got to open our gift.*

*This tradition wasn't just for kids. In the privacy of their room, my parents exchanged pillow gifts too, possibly the most meaningful of the gifts they gave each other.*

**Page 122**

# Bear's Paw Christmas
## Eleanor Burns

*32½" x 32½" Find pattern in back of book.*

## Supplies

6½" Triangle Square Up Ruler

## Yardage and Cutting

| Background | ¾ yd |
|---|---|

Small Claws (2) 6" squares
Large Claws (2) 8" squares
Paws (4) 4½" squares
Corners, Center, and Dividing Strip (9) 3½" squares
First Border (3) 2" strips

| Claws | ¼ yd |
|---|---|

Small Claws (2) 6" squares
Large Claws (2) 8" squares
Corners (4) 2½" squares

| Dividing Strips | ⅛ yd |
|---|---|

(4) 3½" x 6½"

| Folded Border | ¼ yd |
|---|---|

(4) 1¼" strips

| Border and Binding | 1 yd |
|---|---|

(4) 4½" strips
(4) 3" strips

| Bear Applique | |
|---|---|

Tree (1) 8" x 11"
Trunk (1) 2" x 3"
Bear (1) 6" x 9"
Hat (1) 3½" square
Fur (1) 2½" square

| Paper Backed Fusing | ½ yd |
|---|---|

| Backing | 1 yd |
|---|---|

| Batting | 36" x 36" |
|---|---|

*Fabrics used in this project are from Eleanor's Yours Truly Holiday line from Benartex.*

## Making Bear's Claws

1. Place two 6" Background squares right sides together to 6" Claw squares.

2. Place two 8" Background squares right sides together to two 8" Claw squares.

3. Draw diagonal lines. Pin.

*6" square*

*8" square*

4. Set up machine with thread that shows against wrong side of both fabrics. It is important to see the stitching.

5. Sew exactly ¼" from lines with 15 stitches to the inch or 2.0 on computerized machines.

6. Press to set seams.

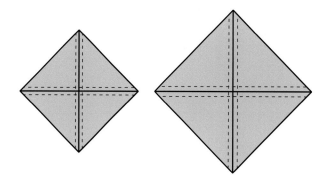

7. Without moving fabric, cut squares in half horizontally and vertically.

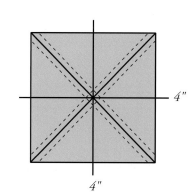

113

8. Cut on both diagonal lines. There should be a total of sixteen closed triangles for Small Claws, and sixteen for Large Claws.

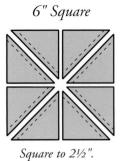

*6" Square*

*Square to 2½".*

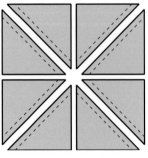

*8" Square*

*Square to 3½".*

9. Square Small Claws to 2½". Square Large Claws to 3½" with the Triangle Square Up Ruler. Press seams to dark.

*Refer to page 12.*

## Sewing Claws Together with 2½" Squares

1. Make four stacks of four 2½" patches in each. Turn two stacks in one direction. Turn two stacks in second direction. Separate.

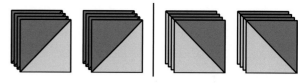

*Stacks are mirror image.*

2. Select first two stacks of Claws. Flip piece on right to piece on left. Assembly-line sew patches together.

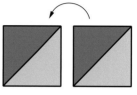

*Make four.*

3. From right side, press seams to left.

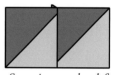

*Seam is pressed to left.*

4. Assembly-line sew remaining two stacks of Claws together.

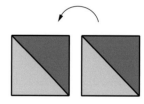

5. From right side, press seams to right.

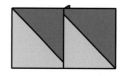

*Seam is pressed to right.*

6.  Stack 4½" Paws with Claws and 2½" Corner squares. Place four pieces in each stack.

7.  Assembly-line sew vertical rows together.

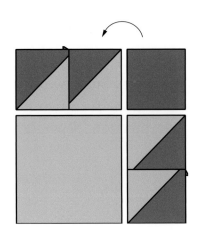

8.  Clip threads after every Paw.

9.  Turn and flip right sides together. Finger press seams on top toward Corner, and seams underneath toward Paw. Lock seams.

10. Assembly-line sew four Paws.

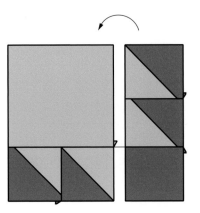

11. Press final seam toward Paw.

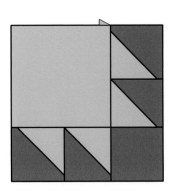

## Sewing Claws Together with 3½" Squares

1. Make four stacks of four 3½" patches in each. Turn two stacks in one direction.

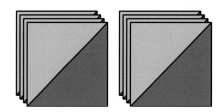

2. Turn two stacks in a second direction. Stacks are mirror image.

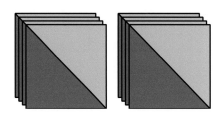

3. Select first two stacks of Claws. Flip piece on right to piece on left. Assembly-line sew patches together.

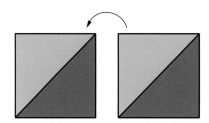

4. From right side, press seams to left.

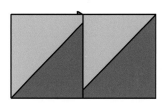

*Seam is pressed to left.*

5. Assembly-line sew remaining two stacks of Claws together.

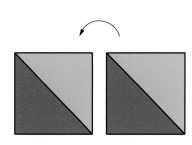

6. From right side, press seams to right.

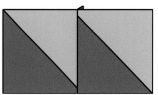

*Seam is pressed to right.*

7. Stack Paws with Claws and 3½" Corner squares. Place four pieces in each stack.

8. Assembly-line sew vertical rows together.

9. Clip threads after every Paw.

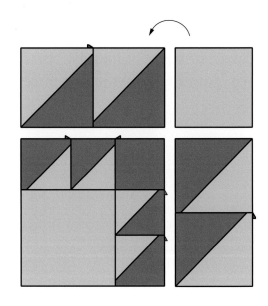

10. Turn and flip right sides together. Finger press seams on top toward Corner, and seams underneath toward Paw. Lock seams.

11. Assembly-line sew.

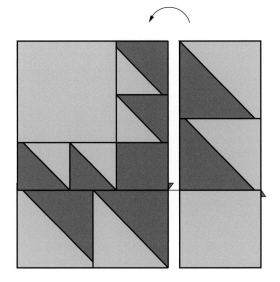

12. Press final seam toward Paw.

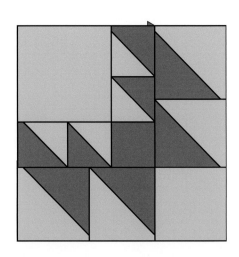

## Completing the Bear's Paw Block

1. Assembly-line sew four 3½" Background squares with four 3½" x 6½" Dividing Strips.

2. Press seams toward Background.

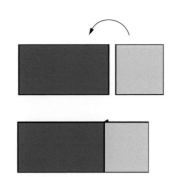

3. Lay out all pieces, and assembly-line sew vertical rows together.

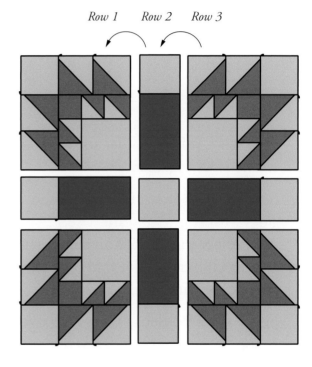

4. Sew remaining rows together. Press seams toward Dividing Strips.

## Adding Borders

1. Sew 2" First Border to block. Press seams toward Border.

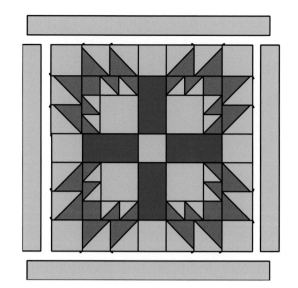

2. Press 1¼" Folded Border strips in half wrong sides together.

3. Sew Folded Border to two opposite sides with scant ¼" seam. Use 12 stitches per inch or 3.0 on computerized machines. Do not fold out. Trim strips even with block. Set seams.

4. Sew Folded Border to remaining two sides. Do not fold out. Set seams.

5. Sew 4½" Second Border to block. Press toward Border.

6. Continue optional Bear Applique on page 121.

7. Turn to **Finishing Your Quilt** on page 196.

## Making Optional Bear Applique

1. Trace shapes on paper side of paper back fusing, leaving at least ½" between shapes.

2. Rough cut around shapes.

3. Place fusible side of shape against wrong side of appropriate fabric. Fuse in place following manufacturer's directions.

4. Cut out shapes on lines. Peel off paper backing.

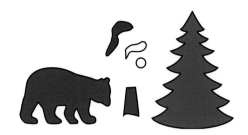

5. Fuse in place.

6. Machine zig-zag or blind hem stitch around shapes with invisible or matching thread.

# Mortimer Moose Wallhanging
## Marie Harper

*16" x 16"*
*Find pattern in back of book.*

## Supplies

⅜" wooden dowel
Permanent marking pen
(2) ½" black buttons
(18) 1" individual craft colored tree lights
36" fine gold wire
24" mini ming pine garland

## Yardage and Cutting

| | |
|---|---|
| **Head** | 9" square |

| | |
|---|---|
| **Antlers** | ¼ yd |

| | |
|---|---|
| **Background** | ⅓ yd |
| (1) 11" square | |

| | |
|---|---|
| **Green** | ⅛ yd |
| (2) 1½" x 18" strips | |
| (1) 1½" x 12" strip | |

| | |
|---|---|
| **Red** | ¼ yd |
| (1) 1½" x 18" strip | |
| (2) 1½" x 12" strips | |

| | |
|---|---|
| **Border Print** | ¼ yd |
| (4) 3½" x 11" strips | |

| | |
|---|---|
| **Interfacing** | ¼ yd |
| Non-woven fusible interfacing | |

| | |
|---|---|
| **Backing and Binding** | ¾ yd |
| (1) 18" square | |
| (2) 3" strips | |
| (1) 1½" x 6" strip | |

| | |
|---|---|
| **Batting** | 18" square |

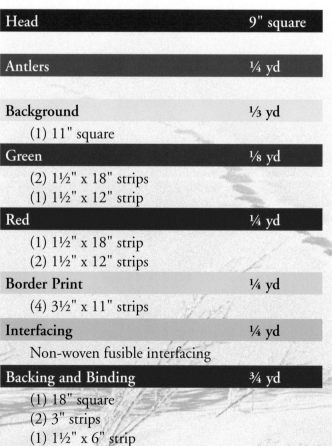

## Making Nine-Patches

1. Lay out 1½" strips of red with 1½" strips of green.

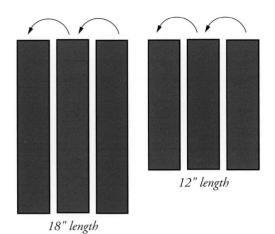

*18" length*

*12" length*

2. Sew all strips together.

3. Press seams away from red.

4. Cut each set into 1½" sections.

*Cut eight*          *Cut four*

5. Sew together into four Nine-Patches.

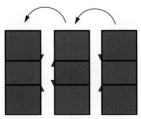

6. Press toward green.

7. Sew a Nine-Patch square to each end of two 3½" x 11" Border Print strips.

8. Press toward Border Print.

9. Sew Border Print to sides of 11" Background. Press seams toward Print.

10. Sew strips to top and bottom, matching seams. Press toward outside edge.

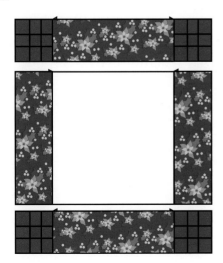

## Get Ready to Machine Quilt

1. Sandwich 18" square batting between top and backing fabric. Pin.

2. Using a darning foot, free motion a meandering stitch called stippling, on Background. *Stay within the center area.*

3. Change to a walking foot and stitch in the ditch around Nine-Patch and Border.

## Making Mortimer Moose

1. With permanent marking pen, trace moose pattern onto smooth side of non-woven fusible interfacing. Place rough, fusible side of interfacing against right side of head fabric.

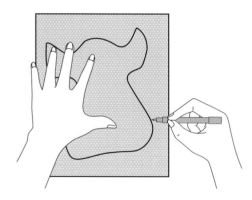

2. Sew on line around moose head with 20 stitches per inch or 1.8 on computerized machines. Trim ⅛" away. Slit interfacing in the center and carefully turn piece right side out.

3. With permanent marking pen, trace antlers on smooth side of non-woven fusible interfacing. Place rough side of fusible on right side of antler fabric.

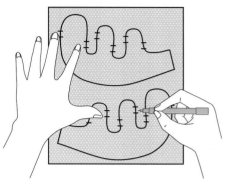

4. Sew on lines. Do not sew end of antlers. Trim ⅛" away. Turn right side out through antler end.

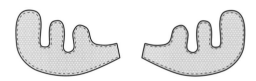

5. Position the finished Head and Antlers on center square cock-eyed. This adds to his personality.

6. Fuse in place with steam. Hand sew with hidden stitches around the Head, leaving the crown open.

*Leave open*

7. On the Antlers, hand stitch with hidden stitches. Remember to leave ½" spaces open (marked on pattern piece) with no stitching. These spaces give you a place to thread pine garland.

## Making Two Hanging Loops

1. Fold one 1½" x 6" piece of fabric in half lengthwise to middle. Fold again into middle and press.

2. Stitch lengthwise along open end.

3. Cut in half.

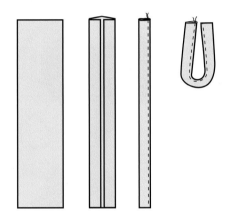

4. Hand stitch the raw ends to back of wallhanging about 2" down from top and 2" from both edges. Keep even.

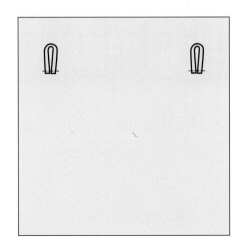

5. For binding, turn to page 201.

## Adding Final Touches

1. Secure black button eyes in a jocular fashion. Add two nose stitches with black thread.

2. Cut two 12" pieces of pine garland. Starting in the middle of head, tuck one end into crown. Loop and weave greenery through open spaces for a pleasing affect with the end of the antlers your destination. Tuck end into the last open space. Repeat on the other side.

3. Secure lights to garland with pieces of fine gold wire.

4. Slip dowel through loops. Hang and enjoy.

# Cold Hands, Warm Heart
## Anne Dease

## Yardage and Cutting

| Background | ⅓ yd |
| --- | --- |

Hearts
- (2) 3½" squares
- (1) 2" strip cut into
    - (4) 2" squares

Mittens
- (8) 2" squares
- (2) 2" x 3" rectangles
- (4) 1½" x 2" rectangles

Framing Border
- (2) 2" strips cut into
    - (2) 2" x 22"
    - (2) 2" x 6½"
    - (2) 2" x 9½"

| Heart | ⅛ yd |
| --- | --- |

- (1) 3½" x 6½" rectangle
- (2) 3½" squares

| Mittens and Binding | ½ yd |
| --- | --- |

- (2) 5" x 5½" rectangles
- (2) 2" x 3" rectangles
- (3) 3" strips

| Cuff | ⅛ yd |
| --- | --- |

- (2) 1½" x 3½" rectangles

| Border | ⅓ yd |
| --- | --- |

- (3) 3" strips

| Batting | 18" x 32" |
| --- | --- |

| Backing | ⅝ yd |
| --- | --- |

## Supplies

1⅛ yds cording or yarn

Two holiday embellishments

Buttons and bells *(optional)*

*14" x 28"*

## Making Heart

1. Mark wrong side of two 3½"
   Background squares and four 2"
   Background squares with one diagonal
   line.

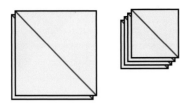

5. Trim ¼" seams.

2. Place one 3½" Background square
   right sides together to corner of
   3½" x 6½" Heart.

3. Place one 2" Background square right
   sides together to corner of 3½" Heart
   square. Make two.

4. Assembly-line sew on diagonal lines.

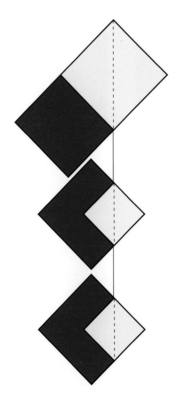

6. Open, and press seams toward
   Background.

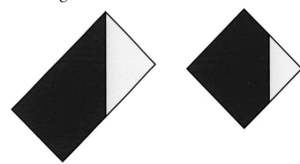

7. Place 3½"
   Background
   square on
   opposite side
   of 3½" x 6½"
   Heart.

8. Repeat with 2"
   Background
   squares on
   3½" Heart
   squares. Make
   two.

9. Assembly-line
   sew on diagonal
   lines.

10. Trim and press.

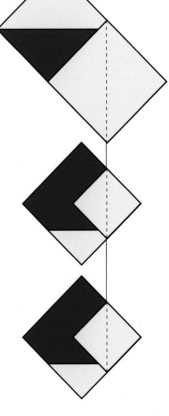

11. Pin and sew top of Heart together. Press seam open.

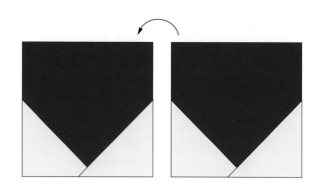

12. Sew top to bottom.

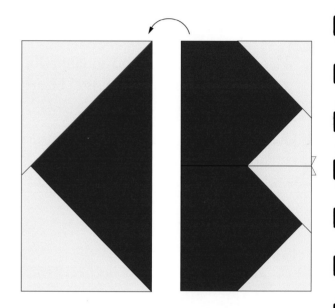

13. Press seam toward top.

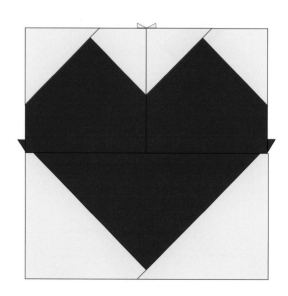

## Making Two Mittens

1. Mark one diagonal line on wrong side of eight 2" Background squares.

2. Place 2" Background squares right sides together with left and right 5" x 5½" Mittens. Sew on diagonal lines.

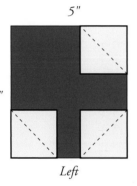
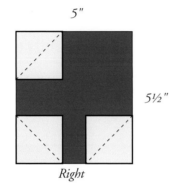

*Left*  *Right*

3. Trim, open and press.

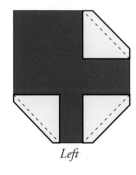

*Left*  *Right*

4. Place 2" Background squares right sides together with left and right 2" x 3" Thumbs. Sew on diagonal lines. Trim and press.

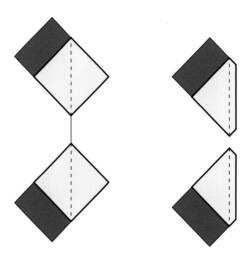

5. Sew 2" x 3" Background rectangles to Thumbs. Press seam toward Thumb.

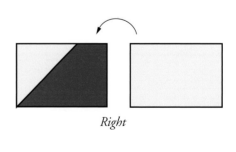

*Right*

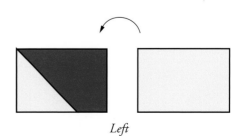

*Left*

6. Sew Thumbs to Mittens. Press seam toward Thumb.

7. Sew 1½" x 2" Background rectangles to both sides of 1½" x 3½" Cuffs.

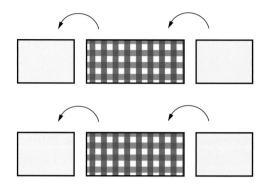

8. Press seams toward Cuffs.

9. Match Cuffs to Mittens, and sew.

10. If necessary, trim outside edges.

*Left*

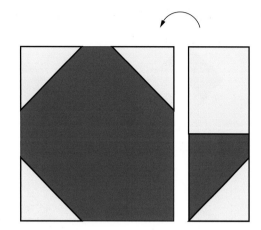

*Right*

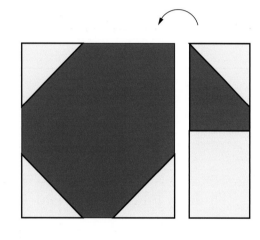

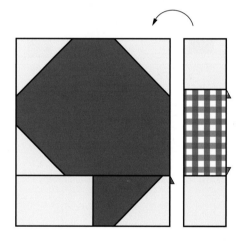

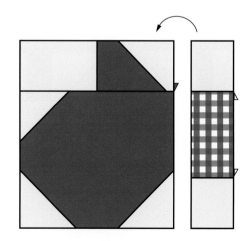

## Sewing Top Together

1. Sew 2" x 6½" Background rectangles between Heart and Mitten blocks.

2. Press seams toward Background.

3. Sew 2" x 22" Background strips to sides, and trim. Press seams toward Background.

4. Sew 2" x 9½" Background strips to top and bottom.

5. Turn to **Finishing Your Quilt** on page 196.

6. Hot glue or hand stitch cord and embellishment in place.

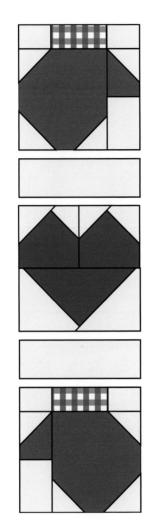

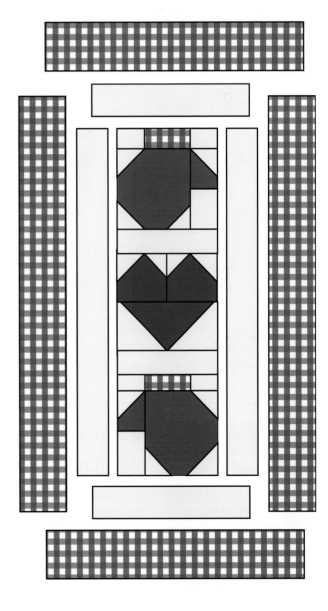

# More Wallhangings

Mary Devendorf

Page 134

## Pine Tree Wreath

*On Christmas Eve, my family gathers at my house for a potluck buffet. Since there are still small children that can't wait to unwrap presents, dinner is a rushed affair. The menu changes from year to year. Sometimes we have lasagna. Sometimes we have deli sandwiches. But, Christmas Eve wouldn't be the same without Strawberry Pretzel Jell-O® Salad. We all take turns making it, but, by golly, nobody better mess with the original recipe! We all expect it and we all devour it. When will one of us figure out we should probably make two? Recipe on page 206.*

Anne Dease

## St. Nicholas Holiday

*Our tradition is one my family brought with them when they immigrated to the United States. Each December 5th we celebrate the Feast of St. Nicholas. The children put out their wooden shoes filled with carrots for St. Nicholas's beautiful white horse, in hopes of finding a small gift in exchange. We now share this joyful tradition with a new generation of children, who are eager to open their gifts.*

Page 140

## Baskets of Cheer

*Holidays are always a time of giving and sharing the blessings we have all received throughout the year. May your baskets always be filled with joy and happiness.*

**Page 152**

Sue Bouchard

**Page 146**

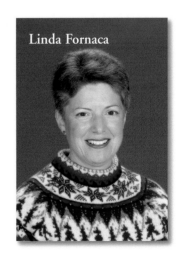

Linda Fornaca

## Reach for the Stars

*About three weeks before Christmas, we would "Adopt a Family" through a program sponsored by our church. Then, carrying a wish list that was hand written by that less fortunate family in our sister parish, we would take our children shopping for clothing, toys and other necessities our adopted family requested. We would wrap the gifts and seal them in large boxes with the name of our adopted family on the top. The boxes were taken to our sister parish where they were given to our adopted family a couple of days before Christmas. It was the true spirit of giving!*

# Pine Tree Wreath
## Mary Devendorf

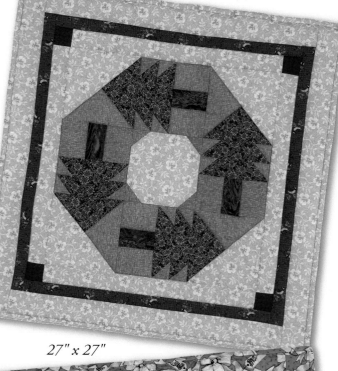

## Yardage and Cutting

| Light Background | 3⁄8 yd |
|---|---|

   **Corners** (2) 7½" squares
   **Center** (1) 6½" square
   **Lattice** (4) 2" x 18½" strips

| Tree | ¼ yd |
|---|---|

   (1) 8" square
   (8) 2" x 6½" rectangles

| Wreath | ¼ yd |
|---|---|

   (1) 8" square
   (2) 2¾" x 15" rectangles
   (20) 2" squares

| Trunk | 1⁄8 yd |
|---|---|

   (1) 2" x 15" rectangle

| Cornerstones | 1⁄8 yd |
|---|---|

   (4) 2" squares

| Inner Border | ¼ yd |
|---|---|

   (4) 1½" strips

| Border and Binding | ⅔ yd |
|---|---|

   Border (4) 2½" strips
   Binding (3) 3" strips

| Backing | 7⁄8 yd |
|---|---|
| Batting | 30" x 30" |

*27" x 27"*

## Supplies

Permanent marking pen or very sharp pencil

6½" Triangle Square Up Ruler

6" x 24" Ruler

## Making Four Corner Squares

1. Use contrasting thread for stitching.

2. Place Wreath and Tree 8" squares right sides together. **Keep Wreath fabric on top.**

3. Draw two diagonal lines.

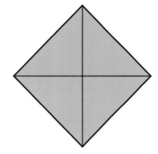

4. Sew ¼" seam down left side of one diagonal line, stopping at center.

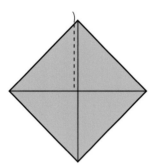

5. Leave needle in fabric, pivot, and sew on center line. Stop ¼" past diagonal line, or approximately four stitches.

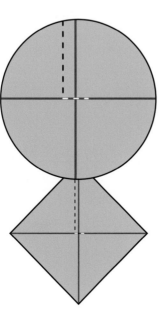

6. Pivot again and stitch ¼" from right side of diagonal line.

*It may be helpful to draw ¼" stitching line.*

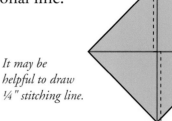

7. Turn. Repeat on second diagonal line.

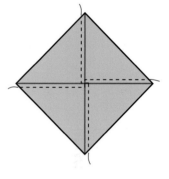

8. Cut apart on both drawn diagonal lines.

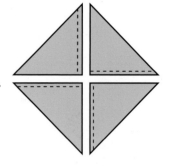

9. Set seams with dark Tree on top.

10. Open, and press toward Tree.

135

## Squaring Up 6½" Patches

1. Cut two 7½" light Background squares in half on diagonal.

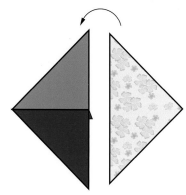

2. Lay Background triangles on top of Wreath triangles, right sides together.

3. Keeping points aligned, assembly-line sew.

4. Place Triangle Square Up Ruler's 6½" diagonal line on horizontal stitching line. Place ruler's vertical line on vertical seam. Trim two sides.

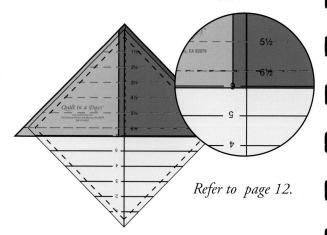

*Refer to page 12.*

5. Open and check first trimmed patch to see if it measures 6½" square. Square all patches.

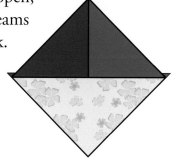

6. Set seams, open, and press seams toward dark.

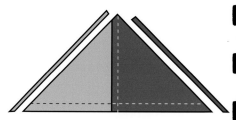

7. Trim tips with rotary cutter or scissors.

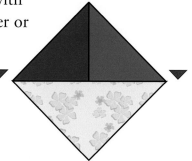

## Making Four Tree Branches

1. Draw diagonal line on wrong side of sixteen 2" Wreath squares.

2. Lay one square on each end of 2" x 6½" Tree rectangles. Sew **on** diagonal lines.

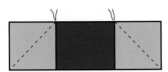

3. Place ¼" line on 6" x 12" Ruler on stitching line. Trim seams to ¼".

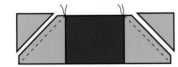

4. Press seams toward corners.

5. Sew two Branch pieces together.

6. Press seam toward bottom of Tree.

7. Repeat for all four Trees.

## Making Four Trunk Sections

1. Sew 2" x 15" Trunk between two 2¾" x 15" Wreath rectangles.

2. Press seams toward Trunk.

3. Cut into four 3½" x 6½" sections.

4. Sew Trunk pieces to Branch.

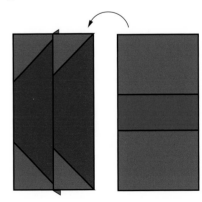

5. Repeat for all four Trees.

6. Press seams toward Trunk.

## Making One Center Block

1. Draw diagonal line on wrong side of four 2" Wreath squares.

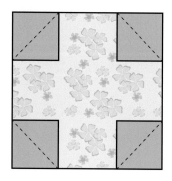

2. Stack 2" squares on corners of 6½" Background square.

3. Sew on diagonal lines.

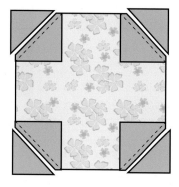

4. Trim seams to ¼".

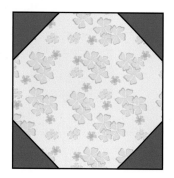

5. Press toward corners.

## Sewing Quilt Top Together

1. Lat out blocks.

2. Flip middle vertical row right sides together to vertical row on left, and assembly-line sew.

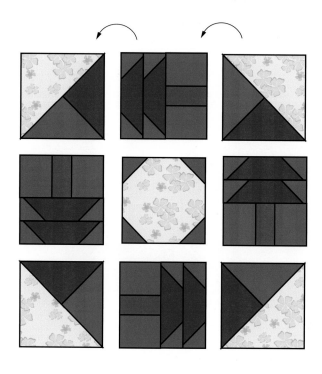

3. Assembly-line sew right vertical row to middle row.

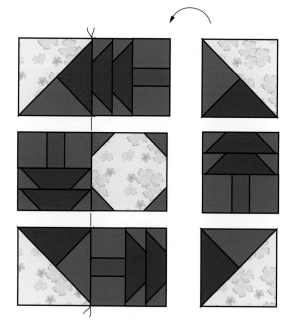

4. Sew remaining seams, pressing seams toward Tree Branches.

5. Press last seams toward center.

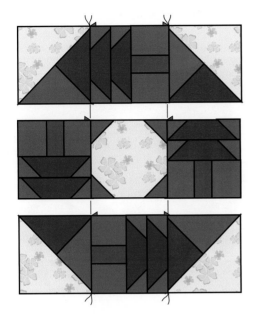

## Sewing Lattice to Quilt Block

1. Sew two 2" x 18½" Background strips to opposite sides of block.

2. Press seams toward Background.

3. Sew four 2" Cornerstone squares to ends of remaining strips. Press seams toward Background.

4. Sew strips to remaining sides of quilt top.

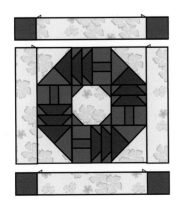

5. Press seams toward Background.

## Sewing Inner Border

1. Sew 1½" Inner Border strips to opposite sides of quilt. Trim.

2. Press seams toward Inner Border.

3. Sew 1½" Inner Border strips to remaining sides of quilt.

4. Press seams toward Inner Border.

## Sewing Outer Border

1. Sew 2½" Outer Border strips to opposites sides of quilt.

2. Trim, and press seams toward Outer Border.

3. Sew 2½" Outer Border strips to remaining sides of quilt.

4. Press seam toward Outer Border.

5. Turn to **Finishing Your Quilt** on page 196.

# Saint Nicholas Holiday

## Anne Dease

## Yardage and Cutting

| | |
|---|---|
| **Trees** | ½ yd |
| (1) 8" strip cut into | |
| (5) 8" squares | |
| (2) 7" squares | |
| **Trunks** | ⅛ yd |
| (1) 2" strip cut into | |
| (2) 2" x 11" | |
| **Stars** | ½ yd |
| (1) 7" strip cut into | |
| (4) 7" squares | |
| (1) 4½" strip cut into | |
| (5) 4½" squares | |
| (8) 2½" squares | |
| **Background** | ¾ yd |
| (1) 8" strip cut into | |
| (5) 8" squares | |
| (2) 6½" squares | |
| (1) 3½" strip cut into | |
| (8) 3½" squares | |
| **Lattice and Borders** | 1½ yds |
| Stars | |
| (1) 5½" strip cut into | |
| (4) 5½" squares | |
| (1) 2½" strip cut into | |
| (8) 2½" squares | |
| Lattice | |
| (4) 4½" x 12½" | |
| Border | |
| (4) 8½" strips | |
| **Binding** | ½ yd |
| (5) 3" strips | |
| **Backing** | 2¾ yds |
| **Batting** | 48" x 48" |

*43" x 43"*

## Supplies

6½" Triangle Square Up Ruler

4" x 8" Flying Geese Ruler with 2" x 4" markings

# Making Tree Tops

1. Place five 8" Background squares right sides together to five 8" Tree squares. Draw diagonal lines. Pin.

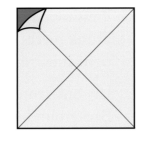

2. Sew ¼" from both sides of diagonal lines with slightly contrasting thread. Set seams.

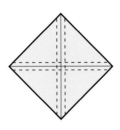

3. Cut in half horizontally and vertically into 4" squares.

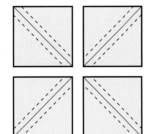

4. Cut on drawn diagonal lines.

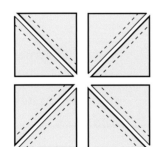

5. Square up forty patches to 3½" with 6½" Triangle Square Up Ruler. Trim corners. Press seams toward Tree.

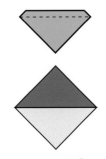

6. Lay out two 3½" Tree squares with two 3½" Background squares. Place four in each stack.

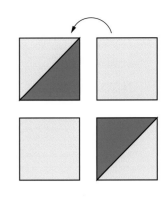

7. Flip vertical row on right to vertical row on left. Assembly-line sew vertical rows.

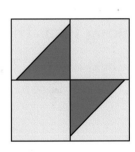

8. Sew remaining rows, pushing seams in opposite directions. Make four.

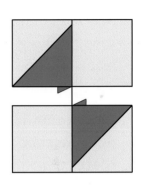

9. Lay out 3½" Tree squares. Place eight in each stack. Flip vertical row on right to vertical row on left.

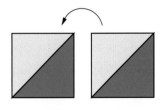

*Refer to page 12.*

10. Assembly-line sew vertical rows.

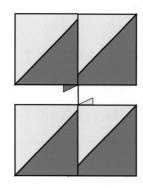

11. Sew remaining rows, pushing seams in opposite directions.

12. Press seams in one direction. Make eight.

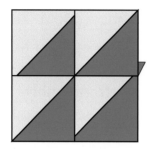

## Making Four Trunks

1. Press two 6½" Background squares in half on diagonal, wrong sides together.

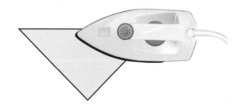

2. Cut in half in opposite direction with the Triangle Square Up Ruler.

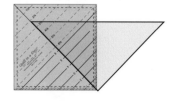

3. Press two 2" x 11" Trunk pieces in half, right sides together.

4. Lay out Trunks with Background triangles on right.

5. Match folds, and assembly-line sew both.

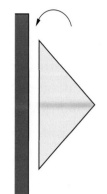

6. Set seam with Trunk on top, open, and press seam toward Trunk.

7. Sew Background triangle to opposite side, matching folds.

8. Press seam toward Trunk.

9. Center 7" Tree squares on Trunk squares, right sides together.

10. Draw diagonal line on wrong side of 7" Tree squares.

11. Sew ¼" seam from both sides of diagonal line.

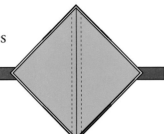

12. Cut in half on line.

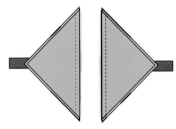

13. Square to 6½" square with the Triangle Square Up Ruler.

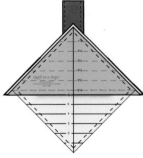

14. Set seams with Tree on top, open, and press toward Tree.

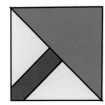

## Finishing Four Trees

1. Lay out 6½" Trunk with Tree Top pieces.

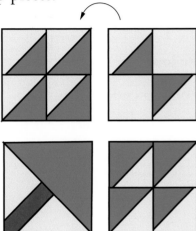

2. Assembly-line sew vertical rows.

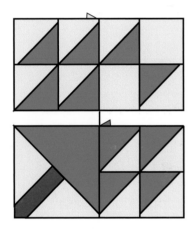

3. Press seams in opposite directions.

4. Sew remaining rows.

5. Press final seam toward Trunk.

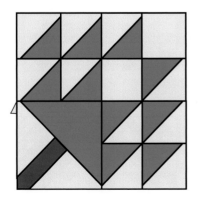

## Making One Center Star

1. Draw diagonal line on wrong side of eight 2½" Star squares.

2. Place Star 2½" square right sides together to corner of 4½" x 12½" Lattice strip. Make four.

3. Sew on drawn line. Trim ¼" from drawn line, open, and press.

4. Repeat with opposite corner.

5. Open and press.

6. Lay out four 4½" x 12½" Lattice between four Tree blocks. If necessary, trim Lattice to same size as Tree block. Place one 4½" Star square in center.

7. Sew vertical rows together.

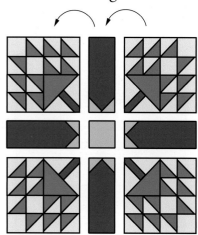

8. Turn and sew remaining rows together, pressing seams toward Lattice.

## Making Four Corner Stars

1. Place four 5½" Border squares right sides together and centered on 7" Star squares.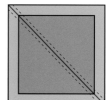

2. Make sixteen 2½" x 4½" Star Points following instructions beginning on page 14.

3. Square to 2½" x 4½" using red lines on 4" x 8" Geese Ruler. Finished size is 2" x 4".

4. Lay out one 4½" Star square, four 2½" Border squares, and four 2½" x 4½" Star Points. Place four in each stack.

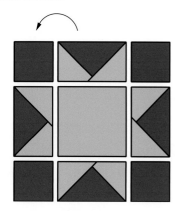

144

5. Flip middle row to left. Assembly-line sew vertical seams.

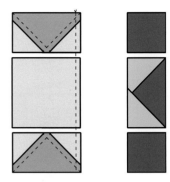

6. Open and add right row. Clip apart every third piece, after every Star.

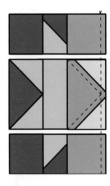

7. Sew remaining rows, pressing seams toward Star Center, and away from Star Points.

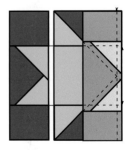

8. Set seams.

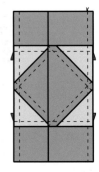

9. Press final seams away from Center.

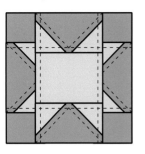

## Adding the Border

1. Measure width of quilt across center. Cut four strips this length from 8½" Border strips.

2. Sew two Border strips to opposite sides of quilt. Press seams toward Border.

3. Sew two Stars to both sides of two remaining strips. Press seams toward Border.

4. Sew to remaining two sides of quilt.

5. Turn to **Finishing Your Quilt** on page 196.

# Reach for the Stars
## Linda Fornaca

*38" x 38"*

## Yardage and Cutting

| Background | ⅞ yd |
|---|---|

(2) 5½" strips cut into
    (8) 5½" squares
(2) 4½" strips cut into
    (16) 4½" squares
(1) 7½" strip cut into
    (1) 7½" square
    (4) 6½" squares

| Four Small Stars | ½ yd |
|---|---|

(2) 7" strips cut into
    (8) 7" squares

| Multi-color Print | ⅓ yd |
|---|---|

(2) 7½" squares
(1) 6½" square
(4) 4½" squares

| Medium for Large Star | ¼ yd |
|---|---|

(1) 7½" square

| First Border | ¼ yd |
|---|---|

(4) 1½" strips

| Second Border | ⅜ yd |
|---|---|

(4) 3" strips

| Backing | 1¼ yds |
|---|---|
| Binding | ⅜ yd |

(4) 3" strips

| Batting | 42" x 42" |
|---|---|

## Supplies

4" x 8" Large Flying Geese Ruler
with 2" x 4" markings

6½" Triangle Square Up Ruler

146

## Making Four Small Stars

*The Large 4" x 8" Quilt in a Day Flying Geese Ruler is used to make these blocks. Use the red 2" x 4" markings for finished Flying Geese.*

1. Place eight 5½" Background squares right sides together and centered on eight 7" Small Star squares.

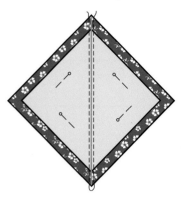

2. Make thirty-two Flying Geese following instructions beginning on page 18.

3. Square to 2½" x 4½" using red lines on 4" x 8" Ruler.

4. Divide the Flying Geese into two equal stacks.

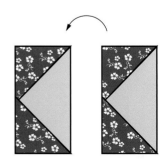

5. Assembly-line sew into pairs.

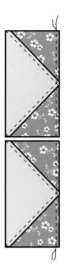

6. Set seams. Press seams from the base to the point.

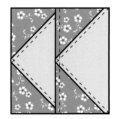

7. Lay out Flying Geese with 4½" Background squares and 4½" Multi-color Print squares. Place four pieces in each stack.

8. Flip middle vertical row right sides together to left vertical row. Assembly-line sew. Clip between blocks. Open.

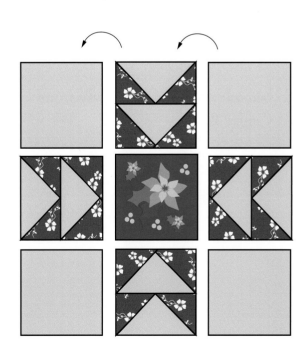

9.  Flip right vertical row right sides together to center vertical row. Sew together.

10. Set seams and press away from Flying Geese.

11. Turn block. Sew remaining rows, pushing seams away from Geese.

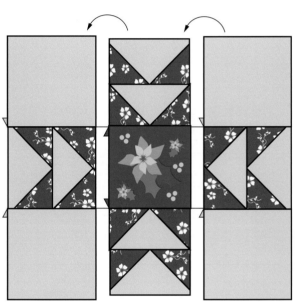

12. Set seams. Press seams away from Center Row.

## Making Center Large Star

1. Place 7½" Medium Large Star square and 7½" Multi-color square right sides together. Place 7½" Background square and 7½" Multi-color square right sides together.

2. Draw diagonal lines. Pin.

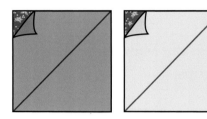

3. Sew ¼" from both sides of drawn line.

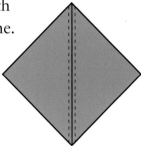

4. Cut on both diagonals into four pieces.

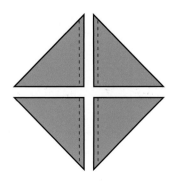

5. Set seams with Multi-color on top.

6. Open, and press seams to Multi-color.

7. Sort and stack identical pieces into four equal piles.

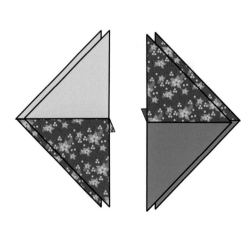

8. Assembly-line sew pairs together, locking seams.

9. Set seams. Do not press open.

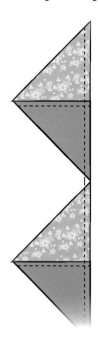

10. Use the Triangle Square Up Ruler to square patches to 6½". Place diagonal line on vertical seam and 6½" line on horizontal stitches.

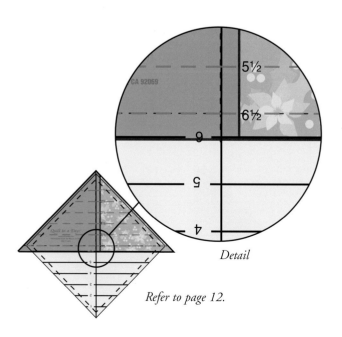

*Detail*

*Refer to page 12.*

11. Trim.

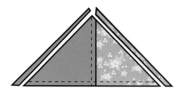

12. Press to the Multi-color/Medium. **Trim tips.**

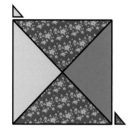

13. Sew four 6½" Background squares to Large Star Points.

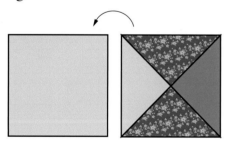

14. Set seams. Press seams away from Star Points.

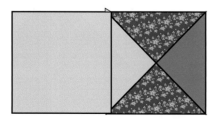

## Finishing the Quilt

1. Lay out quilt top with 6½" Multi-color square in center. Sew vertical rows together.

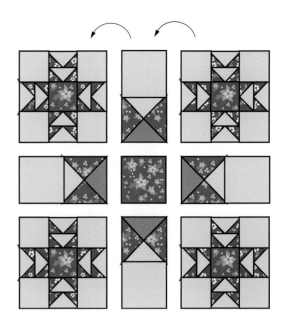

2. Set seams. Press seams away from Large Star Points.

3. Turn and sew remaining rows together.

4. Set seams. Press seams toward the Small Stars.

5. Turn to **Finishing Your Quilt** on page 196.

# Baskets of Cheer
## Sue Bouchard

*Fabrics used in this project are from Eleanor's Yours Truly Holiday line from Benartex.*

*40" x 40"*

## Yardage and Cutting

## Supplies

6½" Triangle Square Up Ruler

| Background | 1½ yds |
|---|---|

Side Triangles
    (1) 20" square

Corner Triangles
    (2) 12½" squares

Blocks
    (2) 6" strips cut into
        (8) 6" squares
        (3) 5½" squares
        (3) 5" squares
    (2) 2½" strips cut into
        (10) 2½" x 6½"
        (5) 2½" squares

| Basket Top | ¼ yd |
|---|---|

    (1) 6" strip cut in
        (4) 6" squares

| Basket Middle | ¼ yd |
|---|---|

    (1) 6" strip cut into
        (4) 6" squares

| Basket Base and Feet | ¼ yd |
|---|---|

    (3) 5" squares
    (5) 3" squares

| Lattice | ⅓ yd |
|---|---|

    (4) 2½" strips

| Second Print | ¾ yd |
|---|---|

Cornerstones
    (1) 2½" strip cut into
        (12) 2½" squares
Second Border
    (4) 4½" strips

| Border and Binding | ⅞ yd |
|---|---|

First Border
    (4) 2" strips
Border Corners
    (4) 4½" squares
Binding
    (5) 3" strips

| Backing | 1¼ yds |
|---|---|
| Batting | 48" x 48" |

## Parts of Block

*There are four parts to the Basket. The Top is made first. The Middle Left and Middle Right are the same except for the direction one gold piece is turned. The Base is made last.*

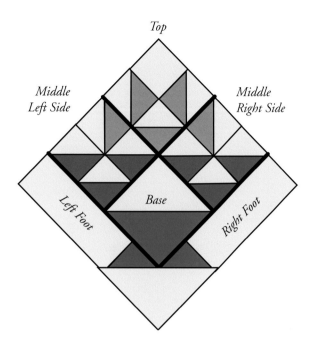

*Top*

*Middle Left Side*

*Middle Right Side*

*Left Foot*

*Base*

*Right Foot*

## Making 2½" Pieces for Basket Top and Middle

1. Place four Background 6" squares right sides together with four Basket Top 6" squares. Place four Background 6" squares right sides together with Basket Middle 6" squares.

2. Draw diagonal lines on wrong side of Background squares.

*Make four.*

*Make four.*

3. Sew ¼" from both sides of diagonal lines. Set seams.

4. Cut squares horizontally and vertically at 3". Cut on both diagonal lines.

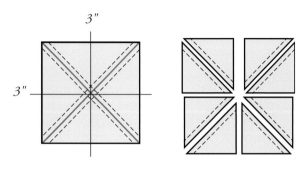

5. Using the Triangle Square Up Ruler, square to 2½".

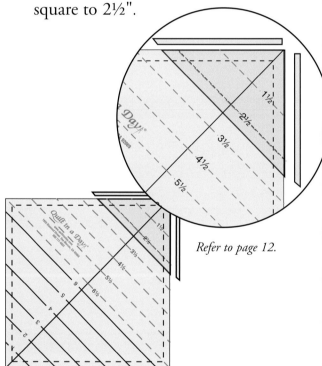

*Refer to page 12.*

*Place 2½" line on stitches. Trim.*

6. Trim tips. Press seams toward dark.

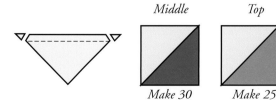

*Middle*

*Top*

*Make 30*

*Make 25*

# Sewing Basket Top

1. Lay out three 2½" Basket Tops with one 2½" Background square. Stack four more on each piece.

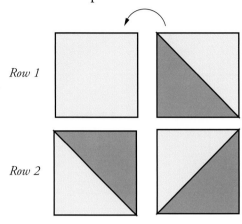

2. Flip vertical row on right to vertical row on left, and assembly-line sew.

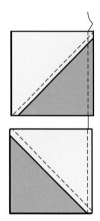

3. From right side, press seams in Row One to left and Row Two to right for locking seams.

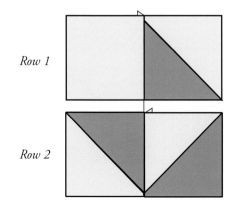

4. Flip rows right sides together.

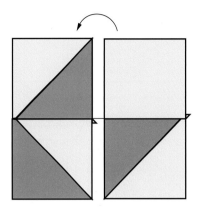

5. Assembly-line sew, pushing top seam up, and bottom seam down.

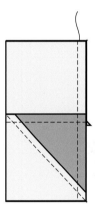

6. Set seams and press toward Row One.

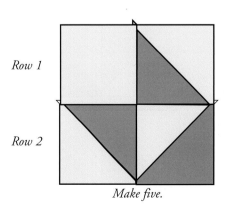

*Make five.*

# Sewing Left Side of Basket

1. Lay out three 2½" Middle Baskets with one 2½" Basket Top. Stack four more on each piece.

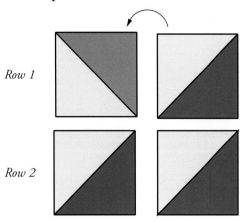

*Row 1*

*Row 2*

2. Flip vertical row on right to vertical row on left, and assembly-line sew.

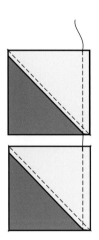

3. From right side, press seams in Row One to left and Row Two to right.

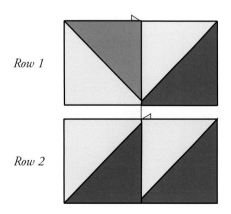

*Row 1*

*Row 2*

4. Flip rows right sides together.

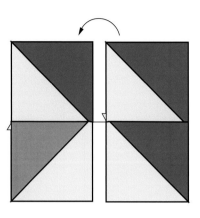

5. Assembly-line sew, pushing top seam up, and bottom seam down.

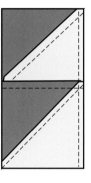

6. Set seams and press toward Row Two.

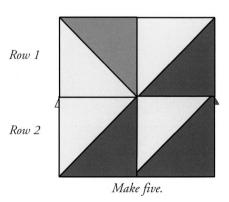

*Row 1*

*Row 2*

*Make five.*

# Sewing Right Side of Basket

1.  Lay out three 2½" Middle Baskets with one 2½" Basket Top. Stack four more on each piece.

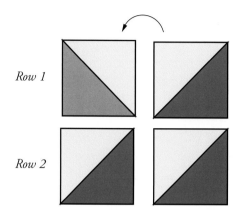

*Row 1*

*Row 2*

4.  Flip rows right sides together.

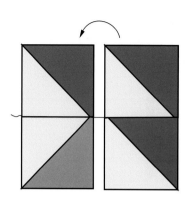

2.  Flip vertical row on right to vertical row on left, and assembly-line sew.

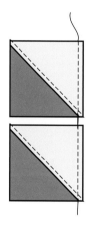

5.  Assembly-line sew, pushing top seam up, and bottom seam down.

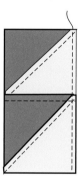

3.  From right side, press seams in Row One to left and Row Two to right.

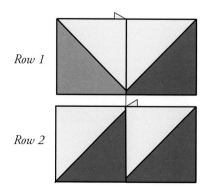

*Row 1*

*Row 2*

6.  Set seams and press toward Row Two.

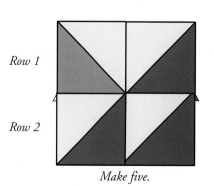

*Row 1*

*Row 2*

*Make five.*

## Making 4½" Basket Base

1. Place three Background 5" squares right sides together with three Basket Base 5" squares.

2. Draw one diagonal line on wrong side of Background square. Sew ¼" from both sides of diagonal line.

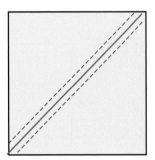

3. Set seams. Cut apart on drawn line.

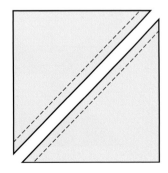

4. Using Triangle Square Up Ruler, square to 4½".

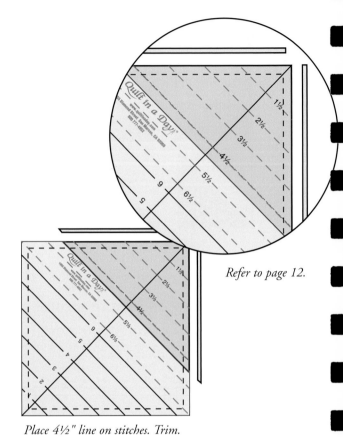

*Refer to page 12.*

*Place 4½" line on stitches. Trim.*

5. Trim tips. Press seams toward dark.

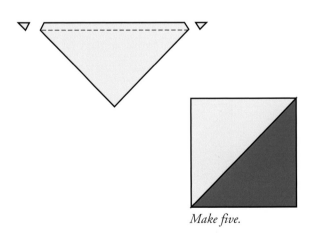

*Make five.*

## Finishing the Basket

1. Lay out Top, Right, Left and 4½" Base of Basket. Stack four more on each unit.

2. Flip row on right to row on left, and assembly-line sew.

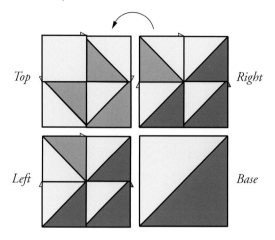

3. From right side, press Row One to left and Row Two to right.

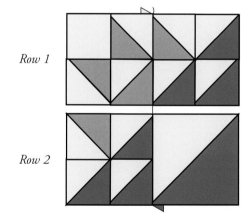

4. Sew remaining rows together. Push top seam up and bottom seam down.

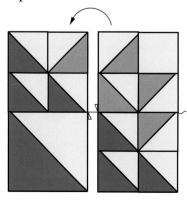

5. Set seams and press toward Row Two.

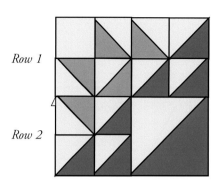

## Adding Feet

1. Cut five 3" squares in half on one diagonal. Sew Feet to ends of ten 2½" x 6½" Side pieces. They are mirror image.

2. Press seams toward Feet.

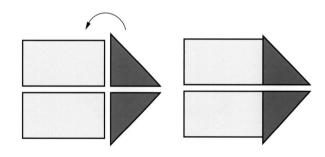

3. Sew one Foot to right side of Basket.

4. Press seams away from Basket.

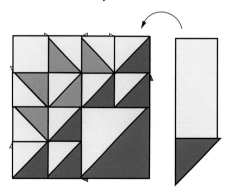

5. Trim tip even with Base.

159

6. Sew remaining Foot to left side of Basket.

7. Press seam away from Basket.

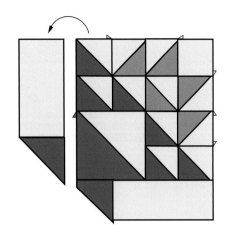

8. Trim off bottom, leaving a ¼" seam from Basket Base, and trimmed to edges on Feet.

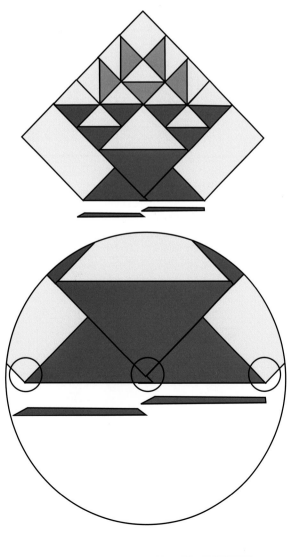

9. Cut three 5½" Background squares in half on one diagonal.

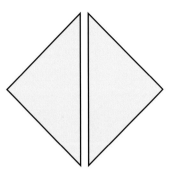

10. Center and sew triangle to bottom of Basket. Press seam away from Basket.

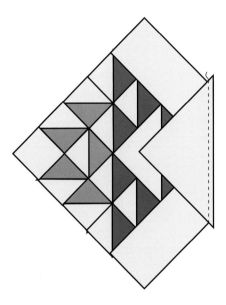

11. Trim excess Background from base of Basket, leaving ¼" seam on both Feet.

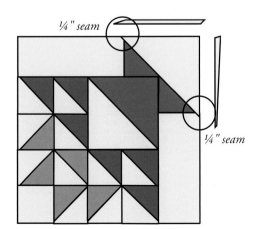

¼" seam

¼" seam

## Cutting Lattice

1. Measure blocks.
   *They should be about 10½" square.*

2. Cut sixteen Lattice 2½" x size of block.

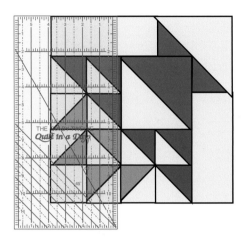

## Putting Top Together

1. Lay out blocks with Lattice and Cornerstones.

Row 1

Row 2

Row 3

2. Sew Lattice and Cornerstones to Rows One and Three.

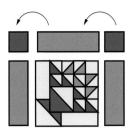

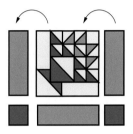

3. Press seams toward Lattice.

4. Cut one 20" Background square for Side Triangles on both diagonals.

5. Lay out a Side Triangle on both sides of Rows One and Three.

6. Sew, and press toward Lattice.

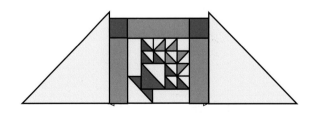

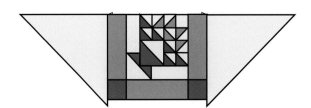

7. Sew Row Two together. Press seams toward Lattice.

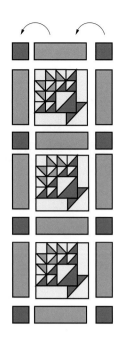

8. Sew rows together. Press seams toward Row Two.

9. Trim excess off Side Triangles.

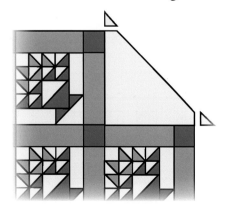

10. Cut two 12½" Background squares for Corner Triangles on one diagonal.

11. Sew to corners.

12. Square up quilt top, leaving ⅝" from outside Cornerstones.

13. Add 2" First Border.

14. Measure quilt top and cut four 4½" Second Border strips to size. Sew Second Borders to sides. Press toward Borders.

15. Sew 4½" Border squares to each end of top and bottom Borders, and press toward Borders.

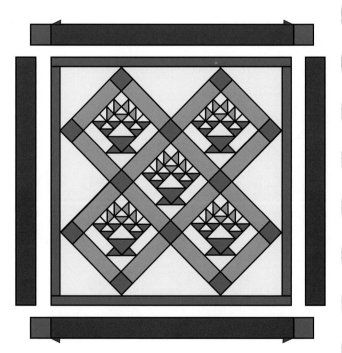

16. Sew Borders to top. Press toward Borders.

17. Turn to **Layering the Quilt** on page 197 for quilting and binding.

*40" x 40"*

With a change of fabrics, the Baskets of Cheer Wallhanging is charming year round. Begin with a multi-color floral print, as the print used in the wide border. Next, pull out all the individual colors from that one print. The color bar along the selvage edge breaks down all the colors, making fabric selection easy. In bright yellows, purples, blues, and green, this cheery quilt will brighten early spring days.

# Quilts

*Fabrics used in all these quilts are from Eleanor's Yours Truly Holiday line from Benartex.*

Page 176

LuAnn Stout

## Rudolph's Four-Patch

*Christmas Eve is a very special time for us. It begins with the family all gathered for a special family dinner. Dessert is an ice cream snowball (ice cream rolled in coconut or crushed peppermint) with a candle in it signifying the birth of Christ. After dinner we have a short program of a story, sing carols, and always end with reading the Christmas story from Luke in the Bible. Then it is time for our traditional Christmas Eve game of Five Thousand. This is a dice game using six dice. It is great because any number of people and any age person can play.*

# Irish Holiday

*My niece, Lissy, has lived in Ireland for the last four years. We all miss her when she can't make it home for the holidays, so I designed this quilt to keep her spirit close to us even when she's away.*

Sue Bouchard

Marcia Lasher

Page 166

Page 182

# Candy Cane Lane

*My great-grandmother was born in England of Scottish heritage. She had four sons. She taught Mom to make "Scotch Shortbread," a simple cookie that is quite delicious. Mom would make the shortbread at Christmas time to give as gifts to neighbors and friends. We would watch her but were not too interested in learning to make it, as I recall. In later years we did get the recipe from Mom, but my few attempts at making the shortbread were disastrous, so it was my younger sister, Jeffie, who carried on the tradition. A few years ago she called me and said if I wanted the shortbread tradition to carry on, I better send one of my four daughters over to learn how to make it! My youngest daughter, Donna, was the one who was most interested, so for the past several years she has been the one to carry on our shortbread tradition. It is a fond memory of Mother and Christmas holidays gone by. Recipe on page 207.*

165

# Irish Holiday
## Sue Bouchard

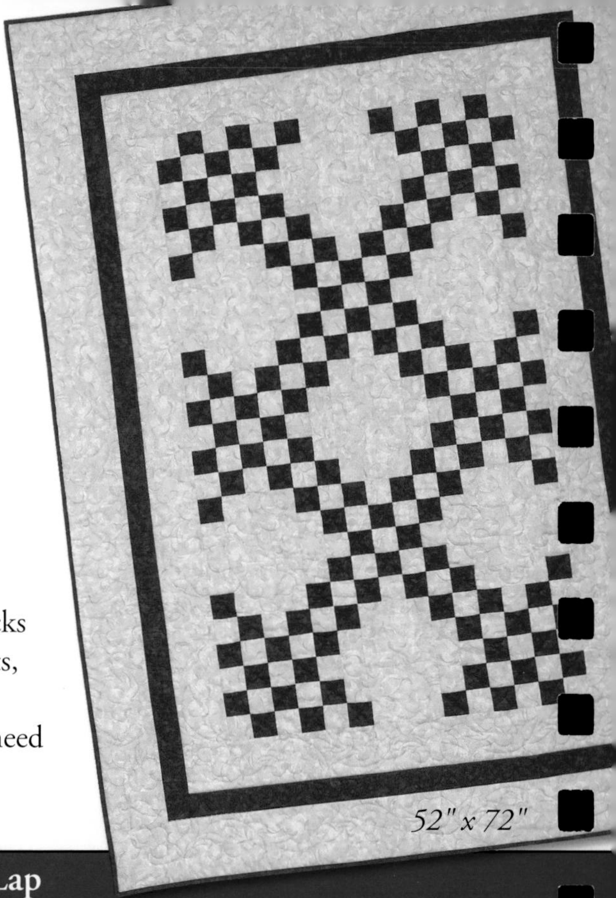

52" x 72"

Choose two contrasting fabrics which appear solid from a distance. Large and medium scale prints do not work very well with this geometric pattern.

Unique to the Wallhanging quilt is the checkered Second Border. The larger quilts have a Second Border made from plain strips of the Chain fabric.

*The Wallhanging also features Holly and Berries in all the B Blocks and in the four corners of the First Border. For the larger size quilts, you may want to put the Holly and Berries only in the corners or eliminate them all together. For Border embellishment only, you need sixteen Large Holly Leaves, twelve Small Leaves and twenty-eight Berries. Use a variety of greens to add interest to the Leaves.

| Finished Block Size<br>10" square | Wallhanging<br>3 x 3 blocks<br>42" x 42" | Lap<br>3 x 5 blocks<br>52" x 72" |
|---|---|---|
| **Background**<br>Chain<br><br>First Border<br>Third Border | 1¾ yds<br>(8) 2½" strips<br>(2) 6½" strips<br>(4) 4½" strips<br>Not Needed | 2¾ yds<br>(7) 2½" strips<br>(3) 6½" strips<br>(5) 4½" strips<br>(6) 5½" strips |
| **Chain**<br><br>**Second Border** | ¾ yd<br>(8) 2½" strips<br>Not Needed | 1 yd<br>(7) 2½" strips<br>(5) 2½" strips |
| **Binding** | ½ yd<br>(5) 2¾" strips | ⅔ yd<br>(7) 2¾" strips |
| **Batting** | 48" x 48" | 60" x 80" |
| **Backing** | 1¼ yds | 3½ yds |
| **Optional Holly Leaves**<br>**Four Greens** | ¼ yd of each<br>(1) 8½" x 11"<br>of each<br>(1) 8½" x 5½"<br>of each | * ¼ yd of each<br>(2) 8½" x 11"<br>of each<br>(2) 8½" x 5½"<br>of each |
| **Optional Berry Yo-Yos** | ⅓ yd<br>(32) 2½" circles | * ⅜ yd<br>(35) 2½" circles |
| **Lightweight**<br>**Non-Woven**<br>**Fusible Interfacing** | 1 yd<br>(4) 8½" x 11"<br>(4) 8½" x 5½" | 1½ yds<br>(8) 8½" x 11"<br>(8) 8½" x 5½" |

*42" x 42"*

## Applique Supplies

Stiletto

Wooden iron

Ball point bodkin

Fat drinking straw

Permanent marking pen

| | Twin<br>5 x 9 blocks<br>72" x 112" | Full/Queen<br>7 x 9 blocks<br>92" x 112" | King<br>9 x 9 blocks<br>112" x 112" |
|---|---|---|---|
| **Background**<br>Chain<br><br>First Border<br>Third Border | 5¾ yds<br>(20) 2½" strips<br>(9) 6½" strips<br>(8) 4½" strips<br>(9) 5½" strips | 7 yds<br>(26) 2½" strips<br>(12) 6½" strips<br>(9) 4½" strips<br>(10) 5½" strips | 8¼ yds<br>(35) 2½" strips<br>(15) 6½" strips<br>(10) 4½" strips<br>(11) 5½" strips |
| **Chain**<br><br>Second Border | 2½ yds<br>(24) 2½" strips<br>(8) 2½" strips | 3 yds<br>(32) 2½" strips<br>(9) 2½" strips | 3¾ yds<br>(42) 2½" strips<br>(10) 2½" strips |
| **Binding** | 1 yd<br>(10) 3" strips | 1⅛ yds<br>(11) 3" strips | 1⅛ yds<br>(12) 3" strips |
| **Batting** | 80" x 120" | 100" x 120" | 120" x 120" |
| **Backing** | 6¾ yds | 8½ yds | 10 yds |
| **Optional Holly Leaves**<br>**Four Greens** | * ½ yd of each<br>(3) 8½" x 11"<br>   of each<br>(3) 8½" x 5½"<br>   of each | * ½ yd of each<br>(3) 8½" x 11"<br>   of each<br>(3) 8½" x 5½"<br>   of each | * ½ yd of each<br>(4) 8½" x 11"<br>   of each<br>(4) 8½" x 5½"<br>   of each |
| **Optional Berry Yo-Yos** | * ½ yd<br>(50) 2½" circles | * ⅔ yd<br>(59) 2½" circles | * ¾ yd<br>(68) 2½" circles |
| **Lightweight**<br>**Non-Woven**<br>**Fusible Interfacing** | 2¼ yds<br>(12) 8½" x 11"<br>(12) 8½" x 5½" | 2¼ yds<br>(12) 8½" x 11"<br>(12) 8½" x 5½" | 9 yds<br>(16) 8½" x 11"<br>(16) 8½" x 5½" |

## About the Quilt

There are two different blocks for Irish Holiday: Block A and Block B. Seams lock when blocks are sewn together.

Block A

Row 1
Row 2
Row 3
Row 4
Row 5

| Number of Block A | |
| --- | --- |
| Wallhanging | 5 |
| Lap | 8 |
| Twin | 23 |
| Full/Queen | 32 |
| King | 41 |

Block B

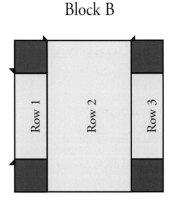

Row 1
Row 2
Row 3

| Number of Block B | |
| --- | --- |
| Wallhanging | 4 |
| Lap | 7 |
| Twin | 22 |
| Full/Queen | 31 |
| King | 40 |

## Making Block A
### Sewing Strip Sets

1. Cut 2½" Background and Chain strips in half on fold. Strip must be at least 21" long.

2. Make equal stacks of Chain half strips and Background half strips. Flip right sides together, and assembly-line sew into pairs with accurate ¼" seam.

   *Checkerboard Border is on Wallhanging only, and strips are sewn with Block strips.*

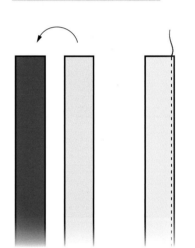

| Number of Half Strips | |
| --- | --- |
| Wallhanging | 14 |
| Lap | 10 |
| Twin | 30 |
| Full/Queen | 40 |
| King | 54 |

3. Set seams, open, and press toward Chain.

4. Divide pairs into two equal stacks. Flip right sides together, and assembly-line sew.

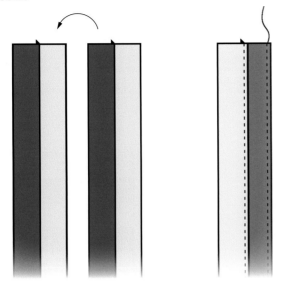

5. Set seams, open, and press toward Chain.

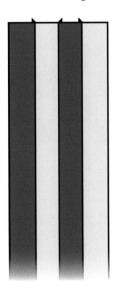

6. Wallhanging Only: Put three sets aside for Checkerboard Border.

## Making Rows 1, 3 and 5

1. Count out strip sets and stack with Background half strips. Flip right sides together and sew. Press seams toward Chain.

| Number of Sets and Half Strips | |
|---|---|
| Wallhanging | 2 |
| Lap | 3 |
| Twin | 9 |
| Full/Queen | 12 |
| King | 16 |

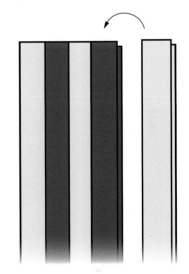

2. Cut into 2½" sections.

| Number of 2½" Sections | |
|---|---|
| Wallhanging | 15 |
| Lap | 24 |
| Twin | 69 |
| Full/Queen | 96 |
| King | 123 |

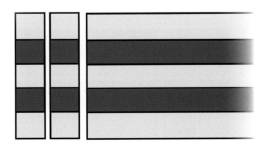

## Making Rows 2 and 4

1. Stack strip sets with Chain half strips. Flip right sides together and sew. Press seams toward Chain.

| Number of Sets and Half Strips | |
|---|---|
| Wallhanging | 2 |
| Lap | 2 |
| Twin | 6 |
| Full/Queen | 8 |
| King | 11 |

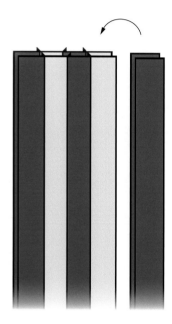

2. Cut into 2½" sections.

| Number of 2½" Sections | |
|---|---|
| Wallhanging | 10 |
| Lap | 16 |
| Twin | 46 |
| Full/Queen | 64 |
| King | 82 |

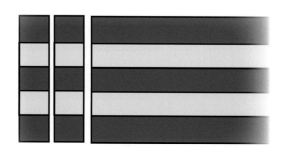

## Finishing Block A

1. Lay out five rows. Place equal number of 2½" sections in each stack.

| Number in Each Stack | |
|---|---|
| Wallhanging | 5 |
| Lap | 8 |
| Twin | 23 |
| Full/Queen | 32 |
| King | 41 |

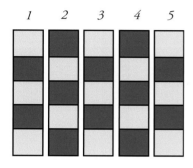

2. Lock seams, and assembly-line sew rows together.

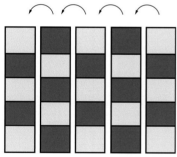

3. Set seams, open, and press toward Rows 2 and 4.

4. Measure and record size of block.

Your Block A Size:_____

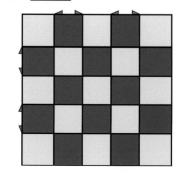

*Approximately 10½"*

## Making Block B

### Sewing Strips for Rows 1 and 3

1. From wrong side, measure Row 4 on Block A including seams against 6½" Background strips. If row measures less than 6½", trim 6½" Background to that measurement.

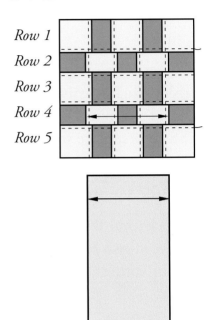

2. Cut Background strips in half on fold. Stack Background half strips with 2½" Chain strips on each side.

| Number in Each Stack | |
|---|---|
| Wallhanging | 1 |
| Lap | 2 |
| Twin | 6 |
| Full/Queen | 8 |
| King | 10 |

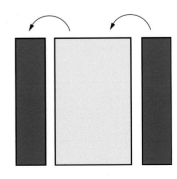

3. Flip right sides together and sew.

4. Set seams, open, and press toward Chain.

5. Cut into 2½" sections.

| Number of 2½" Sections | |
|---|---|
| Wallhanging | 8 |
| Lap | 14 |
| Twin | 44 |
| Full/Queen | 62 |
| King | 80 |

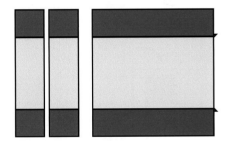

### Making Row 2

1. Cut remaining Background strips into sections the length of your Block A, approximately 10½".

| Number of Rectangles | |
|---|---|
| Wallhanging | 4 |
| Lap | 7 |
| Twin | 22 |
| Full/Queen | 31 |
| King | 40 |

## Finishing Block B

1. Lay out Rows 1, 2 and 3. Place equal pieces in each stack.

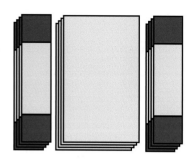

2. Assembly-line sew rows together.

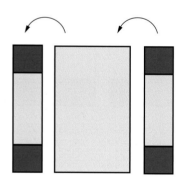

3. Set seams, and press away from Row 2.

## Making Holly

1. Make optional Holly following directions on page 175.

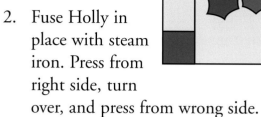

2. Fuse Holly in place with steam iron. Press from right side, turn over, and press from wrong side.

3. Hand stitch or machine stitch with invisible thread and blind hem stitch. If puckering occurs, place stabilizer under block.

## Making the Quilt Center

1. Lay out A Blocks and B Blocks. Alternate between two blocks, placing Block A in four corners.

| Number of Blocks Across and Down | |
|---|---|
| Wallhanging | 3 x 3 |
| Lap | 3 x 5 |
| Twin | 5 x 9 |
| Full/Queen | 7 x 9 |
| King | 9 x 9 |

2. Sew vertical rows together.

3. Set seams and press toward B Blocks.

## Adding Borders

1. Lay out 4½" Background Borders. Sew side Borders first and top and bottom Borders next.

2. Set seams and press toward Borders.

3. Sew Second and Third Borders to Lap, Twin, Double/Queen, and King.

4. Fuse Holly on corners with steam iron, and stitch in place.

5. Turn to **Finishing Your Quilt** on page 196 for quilts larger than Wallhanging.

6. Wallhanging Only: Turn to **Making Checkerboard** on next page.

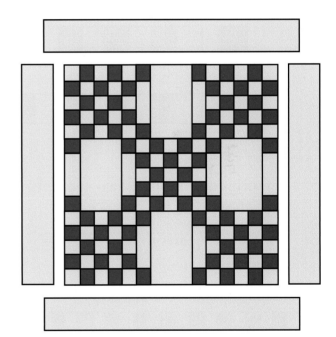

4. Sew remaining rows together. Set seams and press toward rows that begin with Block B.

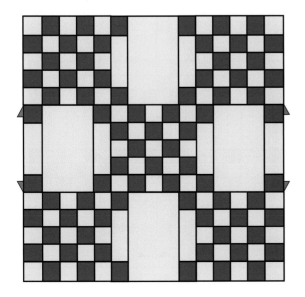

# Making Checkerboard for Wallhanging Only

1. Cut remaining strip sets into twenty 2½" sections.

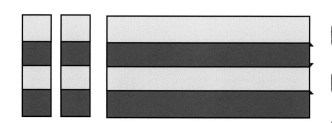

2. Divide into five stacks of four.

3. Sew sections together end to end. Set seams and press toward Chain.

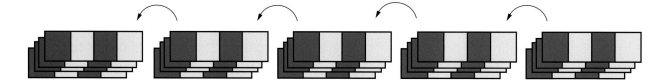

4. Remove one Chain square from two pieced strips.

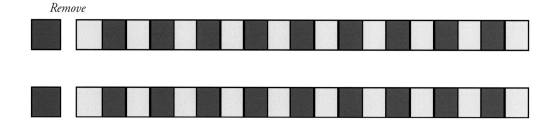

5. Sew strips minus one Chain square to sides of quilt.

6. Sew Chain squares to remaining two pieced strips.

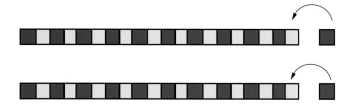

7. Sew to top and bottom of quilt.

8. Turn to **Finishing Your Quilt** on page 196.

## Optional Holly Leaves and Berries

1. Find Holly on pattern sheets in back of book.

2. Turn pieces of non-woven fusible interfacing smooth side up.

3. With permanent marking pen, trace Large Holly on 8½" x 11" pieces. Trace Small Holly on 8½" x 5½" pieces.

4. Match interfacing to same size fabric. Place bumpy side of interfacing against right side of fabric.

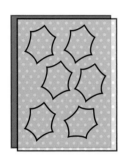 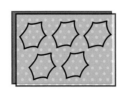

5. Using 18-20 stitches per inch, sew on drawn lines.

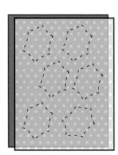 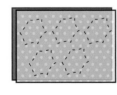

6. Trim to ⅛". Cut small slit in interfacing.

7. Using a straw and bodkin, turn right side out.

*Insert straw into hole toward one end. Push straw against fabric. Place ball point of bodkin on fabric stretched over straw. Gently push fabric into straw with bodkin to begin to turn. Remove straw and bodkin. Insert straw into other end, and repeat turning process with bodkin. Pull out points with stiletto or pin.*

8. Press with a "wooden iron."

9. Trace 2½" circle on template plastic and cut out.

10. Trace and cut 2½" circles from red fabric.

11. Sew yo-yos from 2½" circles. Follow directions on page 39. Stitch in place on Holly through center of yo-yo.

175

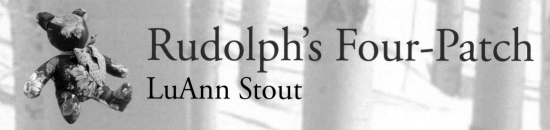

# Rudolph's Four-Patch
## LuAnn Stout

Choose 100% cotton fabric, or for a very cozy holiday quilt, choose flannel.

For Triangles, choose two Background fabrics that appear solid from a distance. Large and medium scale prints would make the pattern look too busy.

For Four-Patches and Solid Squares, choose medium and dark prints. Carefully sort your selection into a stack of medium and an equal number of dark, so finished Four-Patches look balanced. They should have two squares of each, and not be weighted with three of the same value, and one of the other. If you need help sorting, look at the fabric through a Ruby Beholder tool to see value.

Your quilt can be made from your stash. Simply cut the total number of squares and strips needed.

| Finished Block Size 7" square | Wallhanging | Lap |
|---|---|---|
| | 3 x 3 = 9 total<br>5 Four-Patch<br>4 Solid Squares<br>33" x 33" | 5 x 7 = 35 total<br>18 Four-Patch<br>17 Solid Squares<br>46" x 60" |
| **Background**<br>    Triangles | ¼ yd of two different fabrics<br>(1) 5" strip from each cut into<br>    (5) 5" squares from each | ½ yd of two different fabrics<br>(3) 5" strips from each cut into<br>    (18) 5" squares from each |
| **Dark**<br>    Four -Patch<br><br>    Solid Squares | ⅓ yd of three different fabrics<br>(1) 3" strip from each cut into<br>    (2) 3" x 10" strips from each<br>(1) 7½" square from each | ⅓ yd of three different fabrics<br>(1) 3" strip from each cut into<br>    (4) 3" x 10" strips from each<br>(3) 7½" squares from each |
| **Medium**<br>    Four-Patch<br><br>    Solid Squares | ⅓ yd of three different fabrics<br>(1) 3" strip from each cut into<br>    (2) 3" x 10" strips from each<br>(1) 7½" square from each | ⅓ yd of three different fabrics<br>(1) 3" strip from each cut into<br>    (4) 3" x 10" strips from each<br>(3) 7½" squares from each |
| **First Border** | ⅓ yd<br>(3) 2½" strip | ½ yd<br>(5) 2½" strips |
| **Second Border** | ¾ yd<br>(4) 4½" strips | 1 yd<br>(6) 4½" strips |
| **Third Border** | | |
| **Binding** | ½ yd<br>(4) 3" strips | ⅝ yd<br>(6) 3" strips |
| **Backing** | 1⅛ yds | 3 yds |
| **Batting** | 40" x 40" | 53" x 67" |

# Supplies

Shape Cut™
12½" Square Up Ruler

*33" x 33"*

| | Twin | Full/Queen | King |
|---|---|---|---|
| | 7 x 11 = 77 total<br>39 Four-Patch<br>38 Solid Squares<br>73" x 101" | 9 x 11 = 99 total<br>50 Four-Patch<br>49 Solid Squares<br>87" x 101"" | 11 x 11 = 121 total<br>61 Four-Patch<br>60 Solid Squares<br>103" x 103" |
| | ¾ yd of two different fabrics<br>(5) 5" strips from each cut into<br>   (39) 5" squares from each | 1⅛ yds of two different fabrics<br>(7) 5" strips from each cut into<br>   (50) 5" squares from each | 1¼ yds of two different fabrics<br>(8) 5" strips from each cut into<br>   (61) 5" squares from each |
| | ⅓ yd of seven different fabrics<br>(1) 3" strip from each cut into<br>   (4) 3" x 10" strips from each<br>(3) 7½" squares from each | ⅓ yd of nine different fabrics<br>(1) 3" strip from each cut into<br>   (4) 3" x 10" strips from each<br>(3) 7½" squares from each | ⅓ yd of eleven different fabrics<br>(1) 3" strip from each cut into<br>   (4) 3" x 10" strips from each<br>(3) 7½" squares from each |
| | ⅓ yd of seven different fabrics<br>(1) 3" strip from each cut into<br>   (4) 3" x 10" strips from each<br>(3) 7½" squares from each | ⅓ yd of nine different fabrics<br>(1) 3" strip from each cut into<br>   (4) 3" x 10" strips from each<br>(3) 7½" squares from each | ⅓ yd of eleven different fabrics<br>(1) 3" strip from each cut into<br>   (4) 3" x 10" strips from each<br>(3) 7½" squares from each |
| | ⅝ yd<br>(7) 2½" strips | ¾ yd<br>(8) 2½" strips | ¾ yd<br>(8) 2½" strips |
| | 1⅛ yds<br>(8) 4½" strips | 1¼ yds<br>(9) 4½" strips | 1¼ yds<br>(9) 4½" strips |
| | 1¾ yds<br>(8) 6½" strips | 2¼ yds<br>(10) 6½" strips | 2¾ yds<br>(12) 7½" strips |
| | ⅞ yd<br>(9) 3" strips | 1 yd<br>(10) 3" strips | 1⅛ yds<br>(11) 3" strips |
| | 6¼ yds | 8 yds | 9½ yds |
| | 81" x 109" | 95" x 109" | 111" x 111" |

# Making Four-Patches

*Use an accurate ¼" seam. Sew a test set of two 3" strips and measure. Width of strips should measure 5½".*

1. Place 3" x 10" medium strips in one stack, and 3" x 10" dark strips in second stack. Turn all strips right side up.

| | Medium | Dark |
|---|---|---|
| Wallhanging | 6 | 6 |
| Lap | 12 | 12 |
| Twin | 28 | 28 |
| Full/Queen | 36 | 36 |
| King | 44 | 44 |

*Medium*   *Dark*

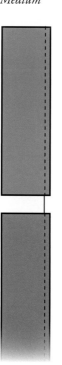

2. Sew 3" dark strips right sides together to 3" medium strips, mixing fabrics for variety.

3. Set seams with dark on top, open, and press seam toward dark.

4. Place first strip right side up on cutting mat with medium across top. Layer second strip right sides together with dark across top. Lock seams. Line up strips with lines on cutting mat, or use Shape Cut.

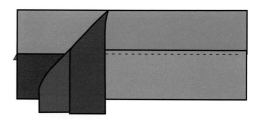

5. Square left end. Cut three 3" pairs from each strip set. Mix strip sets for variety. Stack on spare ruler to carry to sewing area.

| Number of 3" Pairs Needed | |
|---|---|
| Wallhanging | 5 |
| Lap | 18 |
| Twin | 39 |
| Full/Queen | 50 |
| King | 61 |

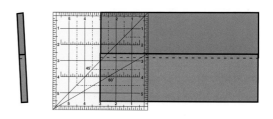

6. Matching outside edges and center seam, assembly-line sew. Use stiletto to hold outside edges together and seams flat.

## Adding Triangles

1. Cut first set of 5" Background squares in half on one diagonal. Turn right side up.

2. Repeat with second set of 5" Background squares.

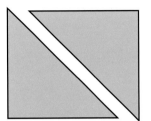 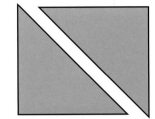

3. Stack Four-Patches into two equal piles.

4. Stack two different sets of Background Triangles around Four-Patches.

| Number in Each Stack | |
| --- | --- |
| Wallhanging | 5 |
| Lap | 18 |
| Twin | 39 |
| Full/Queen | 50 |
| King | 61 |

7. Lay Four-Patch on table, wrong side up. Finger press top center seam to right, and bottom center seam to left. Center stitches will pop open.

8. Press little center Four-Patch open and flat.

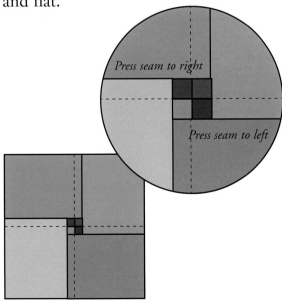

*Press seam to right*

*Press seam to left*

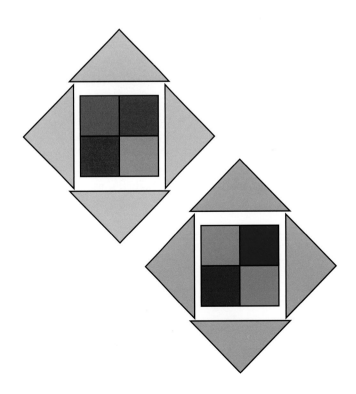

9. Measure Four-Patch. It should measure 5½" square.

5. Flip Four-Patch right sides together to left Triangle. Center Four-Patch on Triangle.

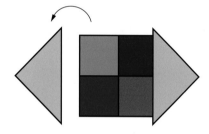

6. Assembly-line sew with bias of Triangle on bottom.

7. Turn and flip Four-Patch on Triangle, right sides together and centered. Assembly-line sew.

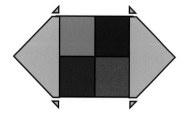

8. Clip apart between blocks. Set seams, open, and press seams toward Triangles.

9. Trim tips with 6" Square Up Ruler.

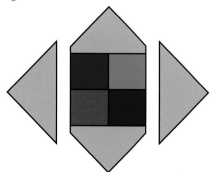

10. Assembly-line sew Triangles to remaining two sides.

11. Clip apart between blocks. Set seams, open, and press seams toward Triangles.

12. Square up block to 7½".

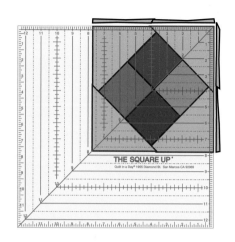

*Place 12½" Square Up Ruler on block. Line up ¼" line on ruler with points on seams. Diagonal line should line up with Four-Patch seam. Trim right side and top.*

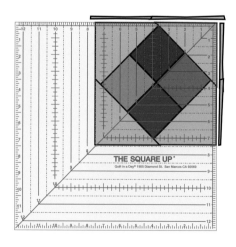

*Turn block. Line up ¼" line on ruler with points on seams. Trim right side and top.*

## Sewing Top Together

1. Count out total number of 7½" Solid Squares.

| Total Number of Solid Squares | |
|---|---|
| Wallhanging | 4 |
| Lap | 17 |
| Twin | 38 |
| Full/Queen | 49 |
| King | 60 |

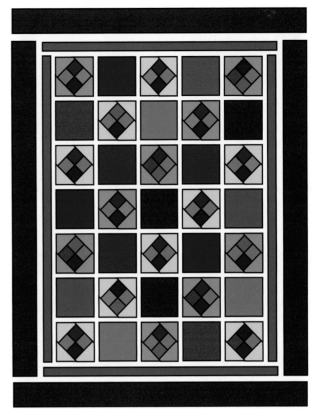

*Example of a Lap*

2. Lay out blocks, beginning with Four-Patch block. Place same Backgrounds in alternating diagonal rows.

3. Alternate with Solid Squares. Mix up placement of different fabrics.

| Number of Blocks Across and Down | |
|---|---|
| Wallhanging | 3 x 3 |
| Lap | 5 x 7 |
| Twin | 7 x 11 |
| Full/Queen | 9 x 11 |
| King | 11 x 11 |

4. Assembly-line sew vertical rows together.

5. Sew remaining rows, pressing seams away from Four-Patch blocks.

6. Turn to **Finishing Your Quilt** on page 196.

# Candy Cane Lane
## Marcia Lasher

## Yardage and Cutting

| | |
|---|---|
| **Twelve Christmas Fabrics** | ⅛ yd of each |

(1) 4" strip from each
*Fat eights are okay to use.*
*Just cut (2) 4" half strips.*

| | |
|---|---|
| **First Border** | ⅜ yd |

(4) 2½" strips

| | |
|---|---|
| **Second Border** | ⅝ yd |

(5) 3½" strips

| | |
|---|---|
| **Third Border** | ¾ yd |

(5) 4½" strips

| | |
|---|---|
| **Backing** | 3½ yds |

| | |
|---|---|
| **Binding** | ⅝ yd |

(6) 3" strips

| | |
|---|---|
| **Batting** | 54" x 66" |

*Fabrics used in this project are from Eleanor's Yours Truly Holiday line from Benartex.*

48" x 60"

## Sewing Strips Together

1. Arrange twelve 4" wide strips beside sewing machine in pleasing order, starting with fabric that will be first block in upper left hand corner of quilt. Divide into pairs.

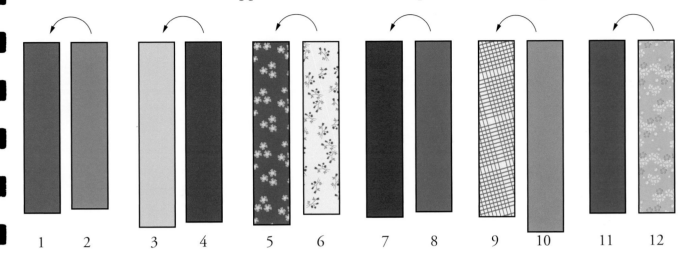

1    2    3    4    5    6    7    8    9    10    11    12

2. Assembly-line sew strips together in pairs.

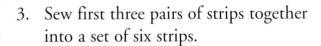

3. Sew first three pairs of strips together into a set of six strips.

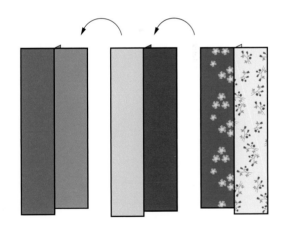

4. Press seams away from first strip.

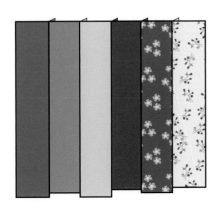

5.   Repeat with second six strips.

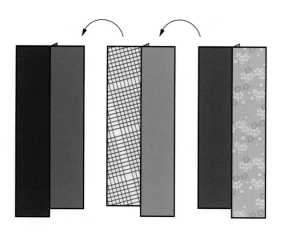

6.   Press seams away from first strip in second set.

7.   Sew both sets together so twelve are in a panel.

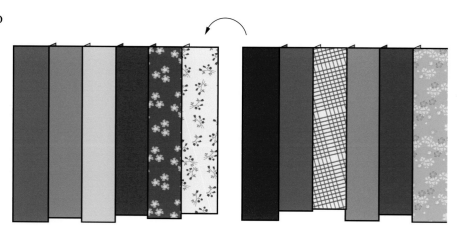

8.   Press new seam in same direction as others.

## Tubing and Cutting Strips

1. Fold panel in half, right sides together, and lay flat.

2. Pin along edge.

3. "Tube" panel by sewing first strip to last strip.

4. Press new seam in same direction as others. Straighten left edge of tube.

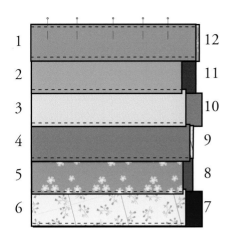

5. Cut 2½" tubes from this piece. You should get 15 or 16 tubes. You will be using an odd number of tubes so the layout looks even at each edge of quilt.

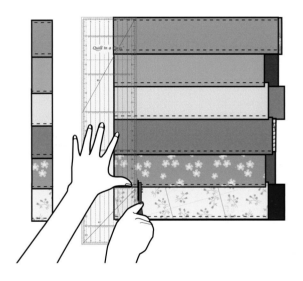

## Sewing Strips Together

1. Find the print that is to be the first block in the upper left hand corner, and the last block, which will be in the lower left hand corner.

2. Cut seam away on stitching line.

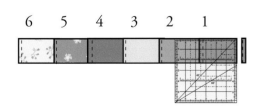

3.  Lay it out on table next to machine, right side up.

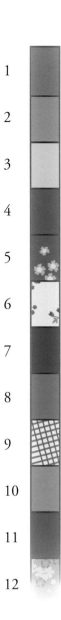

1
2
3
4
5
6
7
8
9
10
11
12

4.  Take second tube and look for fabric of first block. Fold that fabric piece in half, match seams, and cut on fold with scissors.

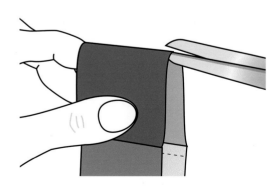

5.  Lay this strip next to the first strip, with the cut edges even to it. Make sure that all seams go down. These half strips are what make up the "Candy Cane Lane."

6.  Pin strips right sides together, lining up the seams of the top strip half-way between the seams of the underneath strip. Sew two strips together.

7. Cut third tube on stitching line of second fabric. The first fabric now becomes the last fabric.

8. Lay third strip next to Strips One and Two, pin, and sew. *Line up seam lines in Strip Three to Strip One before sewing.*

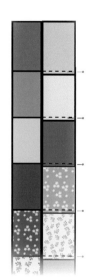

9. Cut fourth tube in half just like second tube, and lay out next to third strip.

10. Sew fourth tube to other tubes, making sure that all seams go down. *Strip Four lines up with Strip Two.*

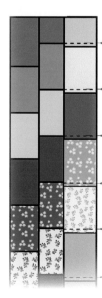

11. Continue in this manner, cutting on the stitching line of one tube and cutting through the middle of the same fabric for the next one, until all 15 strips are sewn together.

12. Press vertical seams in one direction, first on the back and then on the front, to make sure the quilt top lies flat.

13. Turn to **Finishing Your Quilt** on page 196.

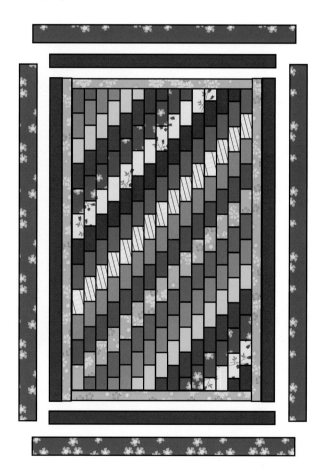

## Hints

*Don't worry if you accidentally cut blocks apart in the wrong place, because you will probably use that strip someplace else along the way.*

*Adjust stitch length on the machine to 15-20 stitches per inch if using flannel. This is a great serger project, especially since seams do not have to meet!*

# Clothing

**Debbie Buckley**

## Jolly Jacket for Fido

*Working at Quilt in a Day was a wonderful time for me, made better by my "special" friends Tabatha and Peanut. Each day they would come into the office to visit and receive a doggie treat. They always brought a smile to my face and warmth to my heart. It was for them that I created the doggie jacket.*

Page 192

*Eleanor's "grandpuppy" Peanut*

## Moose Sweatshirt

*In July of 1994, my daughter Kami and I flew to Alaska for a mother/daughter experience. I'd spent months planning our adventure to take in lots of sights. My fondest wish was to see a moose.*

*The very first day, after renting a car, we drove south toward our first destination, Cooper's Landing. I was keeping an eye out for moose while driving. In a field, way off in the distance, I spotted three brown "things." No one else was pulled off the road, but I thought we should check it out. There, at the edge of the woods, a moose mother and two offspring were feeding. They retreated into the woods as more and more cars stopped at the side of the road. Since then, I've collected moose to decorate my home.*

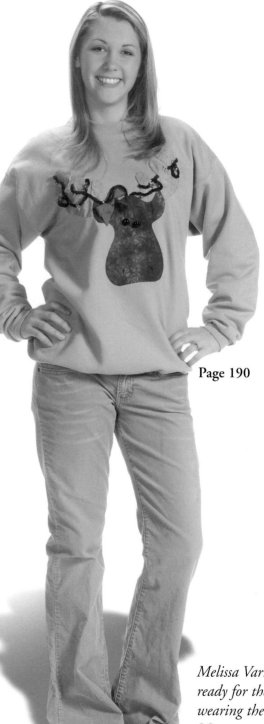

Page 190

Marie Harper

*Melissa Varnes is ready for the holidays wearing the Mortimer Moose sweatshirt.*

# Mortimer Moose Sweatshirt
## Marie Harper

## Yardage and Cutting

| Head | 9" square |
|------|-----------|

| Antlers | ¼ yd |
|---------|------|

| Interfacing | ¼ yd |
|-------------|------|
Non-woven fusible interfacing

## Supplies

Sweatshirt

Permanent marking pen

(2) ½" black buttons

1 yd thick green yarn

½ yd 1" wide red ribbon

(5) ½" Star buttons

(5) washable jingle bell buttons

## Making Mortimer Moose

1. With permanent marking pen, trace Moose pattern onto smooth side of non-woven fusible interfacing.

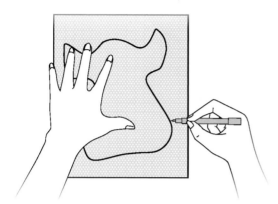

2. Place rough, fusible side of interfacing against right side of head fabric. Sew on line around Moose Head with 20 stitches per inch or 1.8 on computerized machines.

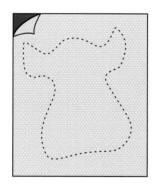

3. Trim ⅛" away. Slit interfacing in the center and carefully turn piece right side out.

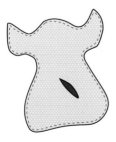

4. With permanent marking pen, trace Antlers on smooth side of non-woven fusible interfacing. Place rough side of fusible on right side of Antler fabric.

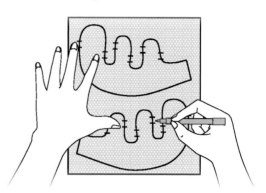

5. Sew on lines. Do not sew end of Antlers. Trim ⅛" away. Turn right side out through Antler end.

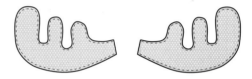

## Position Moose on Sweatshirt

1. Position the finished Head and Antlers on center of sweatshirt cock-eyed. This adds to his personality.

2. Fuse in place with steam. Hand sew with hidden stitches around the Head, leaving the crown open.

3. On the Antlers, hand stitch with hidden stitches. Leave ½" spaces open (marked on pattern pieces) with no stitching.

4. Thread thick green yarn through open spaces.

5. Sew washable jingle bell buttons and star buttons to Antlers.

6. Sew on ½" button eyes and bow.

# Jolly Jacket for Fido
## Debbie Buckley

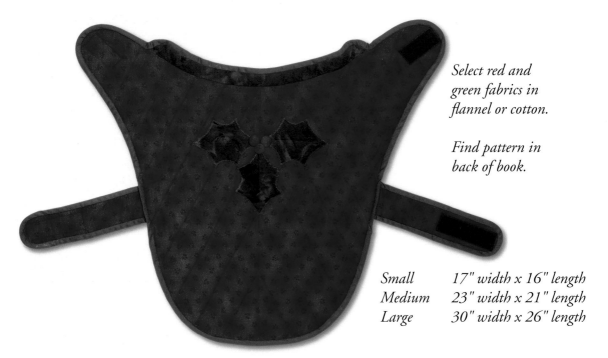

*Select red and green fabrics in flannel or cotton.*

*Find pattern in back of book.*

| | |
|---|---|
| *Small* | *17" width x 16" length* |
| *Medium* | *23" width x 21" length* |
| *Large* | *30" width x 26" length* |

## Yardage and Cutting

| Small | ⅝ yd of Red and Green |
|---|---|
| Front, Lining, and Holly | |
| Medium | ¾ yd of Red and Green |
| Front, Lining, and Holly | |
| Large | 1 yd of Red and Green |
| Front, Lining, and Holly | |
| Fusible Interfacing | ¼ yd |
| Medium Weight Non-Woven | |
| Double Fold Bias Tape | 1 pkg |
| To match | |
| 1" VELCRO® for Small | ¼ yd |
| 1½" VELCRO® for Medium and Large | ¼ yd |
| Red Buttons | (3) ⅞" |
| Thin Batting | 32" square |

## Supplies

Template plastic

Fat drinking straw

Ball point bodkin

Point turner

Wooden iron

Hera marker

*Peanut is wearing a large jacket.*

## Cutting Out Dog Coat

1. Cut sample coat out of muslin to find proper fit for your pet.

2. Lay lining fabric on fold. Layer front fabric on top.

3. Place coat and collar pattern pieces on fold. Place strap pattern beside coat, not on the fold.

4. Pin and cut out pieces.

5. From batting, cut one coat and one collar on fold, and two straps.

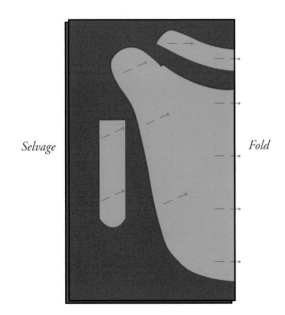

*Selvage*         *Fold*

## Sewing and Quilting Coat

1. Match center folds and placement notches of contrasting collars to coat pieces.

2. Pin centers and notches. Ease and pin layers together. Sew with ¼" seam. Press seam toward collar.

3. Place coat lining right side down with batting on top. Place coat front on top right side up. Smooth all layers together, and tape to table.

4. With hera marker and 6" x 24" ruler, mark a line from center of collar to center of bottom edge.

5. Line up ruler's 60° angle on center line. With hera marker, draw lines every 2½" for large, 2" for medium, and 1½" for small.

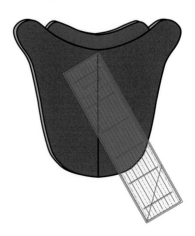

6. Pin layers together with safety pins.

7. Quilt on lines with walking foot and 10 stitches per inch, or 3.0 on computerized sewing machine.

8. Quilt ¼" in from outside edge.

9. Remove pins.

## Making Straps

1. Layer two strap pieces wrong sides together with batting in between.

2. Unfold bias tape, and sew around outside edge, leaving narrow straight edge open.

3. Fold bias tape over edge to back, and pin in place. Stitch in the ditch from the top, catching in the ditch.

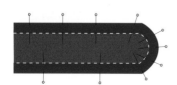

4. Pin straps right sides together to coat lining between strap placement lines.

5. Sew bias tape around outside edge of coat, catching straps in bias tape when stitching in the ditch.

## Making Three Holly Leaves

1. Find Holly on pattern sheet, trace on template plastic, and cut out.

2. Trace three Holly on smooth side of fusible interfacing with permanent marking pen. Leave ½" between shapes.

3. Place bumpy side of interfacing against right side of green fabric. Pin.

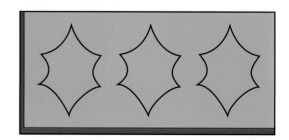

4. Sew on drawn lines with 18-20 stitches per inch.

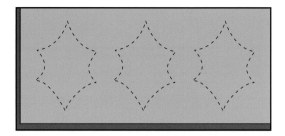

5. Trim to ⅛". Cut small slit in center of interfacing.

6. Using a straw and bodkin, turn right side out.

*Insert straw into slit toward one end. Push straw against fabric.*

*Place ball of bodkin on fabric stretched over straw. Gently push fabric into straw with bodkin. Remove straw and bodkin. This begins to turn piece.*

*Insert straw into other end, and repeat turning process with bodkin. Push point turner around inside edges to smooth.*

*From right side, pull out points with stiletto or pin.*

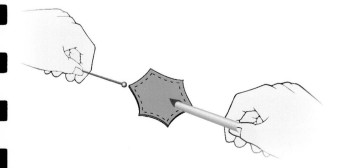

7. Press with a "wooden iron."

8. Place Holly in desired position on coat, and press in place with hot steam iron. Press from wrong side.

9. Hand or machine stitch around outside edges.

10. Hand sew red buttons to Holly leaves.

## Adding VELCRO®

1. Cut VELCRO® into 3" piece and 5" piece.

2. Sew 5" pieces of VELCRO® on ends of two straps for fastening under rib cage.

3. Sew 3" pieces of VELCRO® on ends of body below collar for fastening under head.

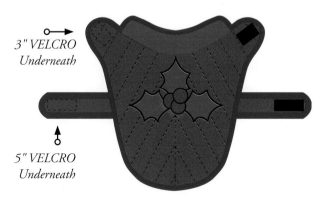

*3" VELCRO Underneath*

*5" VELCRO Underneath*

# Finishing Your Quilt

## Adding Borders

1. Cut Border strips according to Yardage Chart.

2. Trim away selvages at a right angle.

3. Lay first strip right side up. Lay second strip right sides to it. Backstitch, stitch, and backstitch again.

4. Continue assembly-line sewing all short ends together into long pieces.

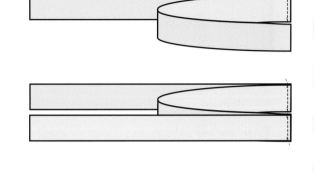

5. Cut Border pieces the average length of both sides.

6. Pin and sew to sides. Fold out and press seams toward Border.

7. Measure the width and cut Border pieces for top and bottom. Pin and sew.

8. Press seams toward Border.

9. Repeat with remaining Borders.

## Layering the Quilt

1. If necessary, piece Backing.

2. Spread out Backing on a large table or floor area, right side down. Clamp fabric to edge of table with quilt clips, or tape Backing to the floor. Do not stretch Backing.

3. Layer the Batting on the Backing and pat flat.

4. With quilt right side up, center on the Backing. Smooth until all layers are flat. Clamp or tape outside edges.

## Safety Pinning

1. Place pin covers on 1" safety pins. Safety pin through all layers three to five inches apart. Pin away from where you plan to quilt.

2. Catch tip of pin in grooves on pinning tool, and close pins.

3. Use pinning tool to open pins when removing them. Store pins opened.

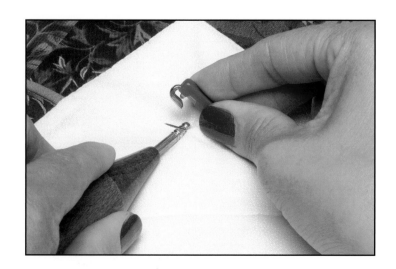

## Quilting Blocks with Walking Foot

1. Thread your machine with matching, contrasting, or invisible thread. If you use invisible thread, loosen your top tension. Match the bobbin thread to the Backing.

2. Attach your walking foot, and lengthen the stitch to 8 to 10 stitches per inch or 3.0 on computerized machines.

3. Tightly roll quilt from one long side to center. Place hands on quilt in triangular shape, and spread seams open. Stitch in the ditch along seam lines, or ¼" away and anchor blocks and border.

4. Roll quilt in opposite direction, and stitch in ditch along seam lines or ¼" away.

# Quilting Blocks with Darning Foot

1. Attach darning foot to sewing machine. Drop feed dogs or cover feed dogs with a plate. No stitch length is required as you control the length by your sewing speed. Use a fine needle and invisible or regular thread in the top and regular thread to match the Backing in the bobbin. Loosen top tension if using invisible thread. Use needle down position.

2. Plan how to stitch, covering as many seams continuously as possible.

3. Place hands flat on block. Bring bobbin thread up on seam line.

4. Lock stitch and clip thread tails. Free motion stitch in the ditch around block. Keep top of block at top. Sew sideways and back and forth without turning quilt.

5. Lock stitch and cut threads. Continue with remaining blocks.

*The advantage to using a darning foot to quilt is that you don't need to constantly pivot and turn a large heavy quilt as you do with a walking foot.*

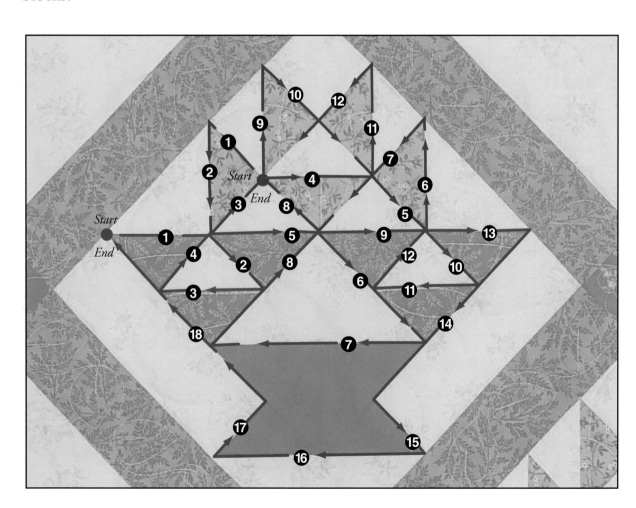

## Marking for Free Motion Quilting

1. Select an appropriate stencil.

2. Center on area to be quilted, and trace lines with disappearing marker. An alternative method is lightly spraying fabric with water, and dusting talc powder into lines of stencil.

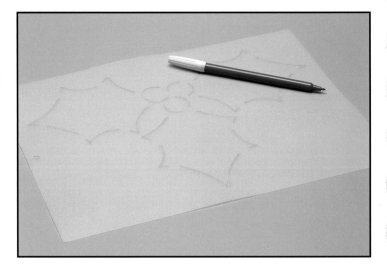

3. Attach darning foot to sewing machine. Drop feed dogs or cover feed dogs with a plate. No stitch length is required as you control the length. Use a fine needle and invisible or regular thread in the top and regular thread to match the Backing in the bobbin. Loosen top tension if using invisible thread.

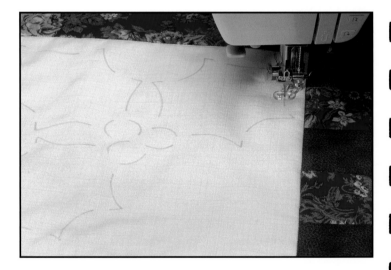

4. Place hands flat on sides of marking. Bring bobbin thread up on line. Lock stitch and clip thread tails.

5. Free motion stitch around design. Lock stitches and cut threads.

## Binding

1.  Place walking foot attachment on sewing machine and regular thread on top and in bobbin to match Binding.

2.  Square off selvage edges, and sew 3" Binding strips together lengthwise. Fold and press in half with wrong sides together.

3.  Line up raw edges of folded Binding with raw edges of quilt in middle of one side. Begin stitching 4" from end of Binding. Sew with 10 stitches per inch, or 3.0 to 3.5. Sew ⅜" from edge, or width of walking foot.

4.  At corner, stop stitching ⅜" in from edge with needle in fabric. Raise presser foot and turn quilt toward corner. Put foot back down. Stitch diagonally off edge of Binding.

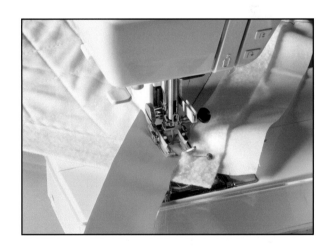

5.  Raise foot, and pull quilt forward slightly. Turn quilt to next side.

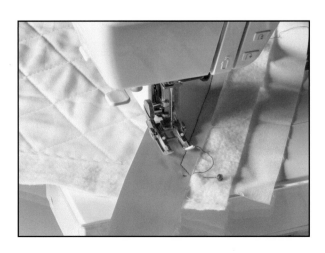

6. Fold Binding strip straight up on diagonal. Fingerpress diagonal fold.

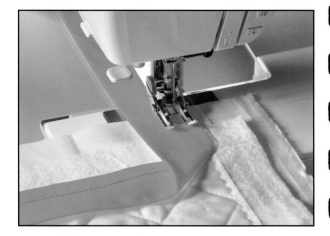

7. Fold Binding strip straight down with diagonal fold underneath. Line up top of fold with raw edge of Binding underneath.

8. Begin sewing from edge.

9. Continue stitching and mitering corners around outside of quilt.

10. Stop stitching 4" from where ends will overlap.

11. Line up two ends of Binding. Trim excess with ½" overlap.

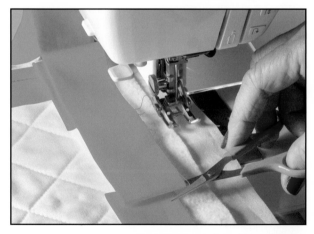

12. Open out folded ends and pin right sides together. Sew a ¼" seam.

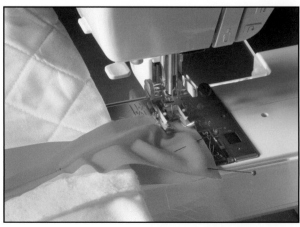

13. Continue stitching Binding in place.

14. Trim Batting and Backing up to ⅛"
    from raw edges of Binding.

15. Fold back Binding.

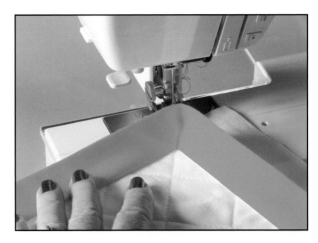

16. Pull Binding to back side of quilt.
    Pin in place so that folded edge
    on Binding covers stitching line.
    Tuck in excess fabric at each
    miter on diagonal.

17. From right side, "stitch in the ditch"
    using invisible thread on front side,
    and bobbin thread to match Binding
    on back side.

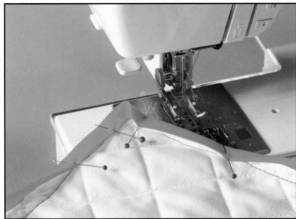

18. Catch folded edge of Binding on the
    back side with stitching. Optional:
    Hand stitch Binding in place.

19. Hand stitch miter.

20. Sew identification label on Back.

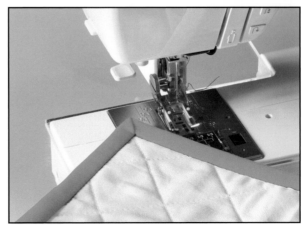

# Index

# Order Information

Quilt in a Day books offer a wide range of techniques and are directed toward a variety of skill levels. If you do not have a quilt shop in your area, you may write or call for a complete catalog and current price list of all books and patterns published by Quilt in a Day®, Inc.

## Easy

Bits & Pieces Quilt
Courthouse Steps Quilt
Double Pinwheel
Easy Strip Tulip
Flying Geese Quilt in a Day
Irish Chain in a Day
Make a Quilt in a Day Log Cabin
Nana's Garden Quilt
Northern Star
Rail Fence Quilt
Star for all Seasons Placemats
Trip Around the World Quilt
Winning Hand Quilt

## Applique

Applique in a Day
Dresden Plate Quilt
Sunbonnet Sue Visits Quilt in a Day
Spools & Tools Wallhanging
Dutch Windmills Quilt
Grandmother's Garden Quilt
Ice Cream Cone Quilt

## Intermediate

Bears in the Woods
Birds in the Air Quilt
Boston Common
Delectable Mountains Quilt
Fans & Flutterbys
Friendship Quilt
Jewel Box
Kaleidoscope Quilt
Lover's Knot Quilt
Machine Quilting Primer

May Basket Quilt
Morning Star Quilt
Snowball Quilt
Star Log Cabin Quilt
Tennessee Waltz
Trio of Treasured Quilts
Triple Irish Chain Quilts
Wild Goose Chase Quilt

## Holiday

Christmas Quilts and Crafts
Country Christmas
Country Flag
Last Minute Gifts
Log Cabin Wreath Wallhanging
Log Cabin Christmas Tree Wallhanging
Lover's Knot Placemats
Patchwork Santa
Stockings & Small Quilts

## Sampler

Block Party Series 3, Quilters Almanac
Block Party Series 4, Christmas Traditions
Block Party Series 5, Pioneer Sampler
Block Party Series 6, Applique in a Day
Block Party Series 7, Stars Across America
Star Spangled Favorites
Still Stripping After 25 Years
Town Square Sampler
Underground Railroad

## Angle Piecing

Blazing Star Tablecloth
Pineapple Quilt
Radiant Star Quilt

Quilt in a Day®, Inc. • 1955 Diamond Street • San Marcos, CA 92069
1 800 777-4852 • Fax: (760) 591-4424 • www.quiltinaday.com

# Acknowledgments

*A grateful thank you to all these quilt makers for their participation in Christmas at Bear's Paw Ranch.*

Sue Bouchard
Debbie Buckley
Anne Dease
Mary Devendorf
Linda Fornaca
Marie Harper
Judy Knoechel

Patricia Knoechel
Marcia Lasher
Dylan Mayer
Linda Parker
Amie Potter

Mercilee Searles
LuAnn Stout
Sandy Thompson
Amber Varnes
Melissa Varnes
Teresa Varnes
Luckie Yasukochi

**Strawberry Jell-O®
Pretzel Salad**

*from the kitchen of Mary Devendorf*

2 cups crushed pretzels
¾ cup margarine or butter, melted
2 tbsp sugar
8 oz. softened cream cheese
½ cup sugar
8 oz. Cool Whip®
1 pkg (6 oz.) strawberry Jell-O®
2 cups boiling water
1 pkg (20 oz.) frozen strawberries

Combine crushed pretzels with melted margarine and 2 tbsp sugar. Pat into 9" x 13" pan.
Bake in 400° oven for 8 minutes. Cool completely.
Cream together cream cheese and ½ cup sugar. Fold into Cool Whip®.
Spread over cooled pretzel mixture. Prepare Jell-O® using 2 cups boiling water.
Stir frozen strawberries into Jell-O® mixture until thawed. Pour over top of cream layer and
refrigerate until firm.

Bear's Paw Ranch, decorated with garlands and wreaths welcomes family and friends for the holidays. The three bears on the deck are kept toasty warm in their Santa hats.

## Scotch Shortbread

*from the kitchen of Marcia Lasher*

2½ cups flour
½ cup light brown sugar
1 cup real butter (8 oz.)

Combine flour and brown sugar. Cut in butter until mixture resembles fine crumbs. Form into a ball. Knead until smooth. Line a 9" x 13" baking sheet with brown paper (For thrifty people, brown grocery bags work great!) and press dough into the pan about ¾" thick. Using your fingers, scallop the edges of the dough. Pierce dough all over with a fork. Bake at 300° for about 40-50 minutes. Cut while still warm into 1" squares.

Snow at Bear's Paw Ranch turns Eleanor's nine acre retreat into a winter wonderland. Located in Julian, California air is crisp and clean at 4,500 feet elevation and 60 miles east from metropolitan San Diego. Raccoon, fox, and deer secretly visit the pond at night, leaving their prints for El's morning discovery and delight.

The Bear's Paw is a perfect hide-away for El's quilting on cold winter evenings.

### Lone Pine Placemats and Any Season Tablerunner – Sandy Thompson

Flying Geese Patches provide the perfect shape for Sandy's Lone Pine Placemats. This project is so quick and easy you will want to make them for your own table and as gifts for loved ones.
To coordinate beautifully with her Placemats, Sandy combined a star and pinwheels with her pine trees for a country table setting. They are the perfect addition to any holiday table.